In Strength Not Our Own

In Strength Not Our Own

A Maasai Medical Miracle

Georgie Orme & Irene Howat

CHRISTIAN
FOCUS

ISBN 978 1 84550 334 5

Copyright © Christian Focus Publications 2008

10 9 8 7 6 5 4 3 2 1

Published in 2008 by
Christian Focus Publications, Geanies House,
Fearn, Ross-shire, IV20 1TW, Scotland.

www.christianfocus.com

Cover design by Alister MacInnes

Printed and bound by Norhaven, Denmark

Contents

1
About turn!

I sat in the auditorium at Kijabe, a mission station in Kenya, frozen with indecision. The Communion bread and wine were being passed round and they would soon reach me. Within minutes I had to make the biggest and most important decision in my life. I had been living a double life for years, living a lie. If I ate the bread and drank the wine it would be because I had surrendered to Jesus wholeheartedly, repented of my hypocrisy and all my sin and put my faith in the One who died for me. If I rejected the elements, it would be because I had deliberately decided to reject God and all I knew of His love and mercy, but I would be through with double standards. It would be all or nothing from then on. I couldn't go on pretending.

I first met Sally Allen and other Africa Inland Mission (A.I.M.) missionaries in Edinburgh when I was a Midwifery Tutor. Sally, an American missionary in Kenya, came to Scotland in the 1960s to get a midwifery qualification which she needed at the mission hospital in which she was working. I had been surprised to learn from her that in the U.S.A. nurses didn't deliver babies, only doctors did! These missionaries intrigued me. I had thought about becoming a missionary on and off for years, but only because they seemed to do a lot of travelling in interesting places and that appealed to me greatly! But I realised I wasn't suitable because missionaries had to go to Bible College, and I knew for sure that I wasn't a fit person for Bible College. I don't know that my unfitness for missionary service ever occurred to me! I had even mentioned the possibility of becoming a missionary to my mother; she wasn't at all pleased because she didn't want me to go away and leave her. But any thought of being a missionary departed when my two worlds collided.

For years I had successfully lived in two worlds, with two groups of friends and two sets of interests. I had my church friends, in whose company I tried to act christianly, and my working colleagues with whom I knew how to enjoy myself. I had even become a church member though I knew deep down that I wasn't really a Christian. I did believe in God, but I certainly didn't live a Christian life even though I did try. Over and over again I started reading my Bible and promised myself I would read it every day and pray; but it always fizzled out. The truth is that I tried to be a Christian by copying Christians rather than by having a personal faith in the Lord Jesus Christ. So my efforts were doomed to failure.

That all came to an end when I had several nursing colleagues home for a meal. We were enjoying ourselves, and the evidence of our enjoyment was everywhere: sherry, wine, liqueurs and ashtrays full to overflowing. Glancing out of the window, I saw my minister and elder walking up the cul-de-sac and I knew they were coming to visit me. Oblivious of my friends, I rushed around the room gathering up glasses, bottles and ashtrays. I can't imagine what they thought when I started to spray the room with hairspray to get rid of the smell of smoke! Then in a moment of revelation, I thought, 'Georgie Orme, you are a hypocrite.' At that point I decided not to go back to church.

It was in 1970, when I was working as an assistant tutor in the Elsie Inglis Maternity Hospital in Edinburgh, that I met Sally Allen again. She came back to do a special baby care course and we got to know each other quite well. When Sally heard that I was coming to the end of my teaching contract, she suggested I consider going out to Kenya and gave me the names of hospitals to which I might apply. Unknown to me Sally soon had second thoughts and was in great trepidation at the thought of me going! She was praying for all she was worth that God would stop me from going to Kenya if it wasn't his will for me to be there. To my great surprise one of my letters brought a positive response and, in May 1974, I took up the position of Midwife Tutor in a Roman Catholic mission hospital in Nairobi. I was in Kenya!

I plunged into Nairobi's social life, enjoying drinking and socialising in the expat party circuit. But the job in Nairobi was enormous, more than I could handle. As the stress increased so did my intake of alcohol and sedatives. Nairobi was just over an hour's travelling time from Kijabe Hospital where Sally worked and I used to go up for weekends to visit, complete with my bottle of gin and a good supply of cigarettes. I don't know how she put up with me. When I eventually decided to go back to the U.K., I went to Kijabe to say goodbye. As we walked to church that Sunday I said to Sally, 'It's a fine thing. I come up here and am surrounded by missionaries but none of you ever talk to me about the Lord.' Sally stopped walking and looked at me. 'If I were in your shoes, I would be wondering how much longer God was going to give me.' That stopped me in my tracks. I thought back to all the times I had decided to be a Christian and had failed. I prayed, 'God, if you are really there, please help me to make a decision to follow you that I cannot later doubt.'

We arrived at church and the service was being led by Ed Arensen, an American A.I.M. missionary. The reading was from 1 John 2:15-19 (AV). 'Little children, it is the last time…' With Sally's words still ringing in my ears, the urgency hit me. It was as if God was telling me this was my last chance. 'There are many antichrists,' Ed said, and explained that 'antichrist' meant 'against Christ.' He emphasised, 'you are either for Christ or against Christ; there is no middle ground.' 'They went out from us because they did not really belong to us,' he read. That was me exactly. I was just like those people in the early church. I had left my church in Edinburgh for that very reason; I had nothing in common with them. I had no doubt who this message was for! Everyone else there was either a missionary or from a missionary family. And there was more to come – the Communion service.

Ed spoke on 1 Corinthians 11:27-29, explaining that the Communion service was an act of remembrance of the death of Jesus, crucified for us. He emphasised, 'Whoever eats the bread or drinks the cup of the Lord in an unworthy manner will be guilty of sinning against the body and blood of the Lord' (v. 27). 'That means taking the bread and wine without truly believing that Christ died for you – you yourself, taking the punishment for your sin on the cross,' Ed explained. He read on from the same passage, 'A man ought to examine himself before he eats the bread and drinks of the cup. For anyone who eats and drinks without recognising the body of the Lord eats and drinks judgment on himself.'

It was at that point I realised I had a decision to make. I either had to repent, turn to Jesus with an undivided heart and take Communion, or not be part of it at all. There was a group of boys sitting beside me and I thought they wouldn't take the bread and therefore it wouldn't look too bad if I also passed the plate on. But they did take it, and I did too, knowing with a certainty as I did so that I had eaten the bread and drunk the wine believing. During that Communion service I was born again and I knew it. God had answered my prayer to help me to make a decision that I couldn't later doubt. I can't; I am reminded of it every time I take Communion!

When I went back to Nairobi that night there was a letter waiting for me from my mother. She had been to a Women's Guild meeting and had heard a missionary describe how she had been delayed for years from going to the mission field because her mother didn't want her to go. Remembering back to her total opposition to the very mention of my being a missionary previously, because she hadn't wanted me to go abroad and leave her, Mum now wrote in quite different terms. 'I realise I am just like that woman, and if you still want to be a missionary, I will be right behind you.' There was no doubt in my mind what my next step would be. In fact, when I returned to the U.K. it was Mum who looked for and found the address of A.I.M. in order that I could find out how to become a candidate! Following that I went to the April Scottish Conference at Bonskeid House in Perthshire, and it was there that my immediate future became clear. I needed to go to Bible College for two years to train for missionary service.

Early years

'Next stop, Bible College!' I thought as I pulled the car door shut. Looking in the rear-view mirror, it was as if I could see my life all packed up on the back seat behind me. It was a long drive south to London, quite long enough to have time to think over the journey that had brought me thus far. It started in 1941, when I was born in the station cottage at Kilkerran in Ayrshire. My grandfather was stationmaster there. My mother went back home to her parents for my birth. My father, who was in the hotel trade, worked in Glasgow. I was named after my grandmother. She was Georgina, and I am too, although I have always been known as Georgie.

My earliest memories were, however, not of Scotland at all. The Second World War was raging at the time of my birth, and shortly afterwards my father was called up to serve in the Royal Air Force as a flight mechanic. He was based in East Anglia and Mum and I went south with him. One day his squadron was marching along a country road when a tank ploughed into a group of airmen and Dad was knocked into a ditch. That probably saved his life as two or three of his comrades died at the scene. Dad's femur was smashed and he spent many months in hospital encased in plaster. My best memory of visiting him there is of chocolate, as some of the men in his ward kept their chocolate rations for me! Dad walked with a limp thereafter. But I think the damage done to him and others by their wartime experiences went far into their beings. Many men like Dad found it difficult to talk about what they had gone through.

I'm told that I had a friend in our old Suffolk gardener. I followed him around as he worked, and my speech developed based on how he spoke. That accent caused no problems whatever as long as we lived in Suffolk, but when Dad was demobbed, and we moved back to Prestwick in Scotland, no one could understand a word I said! Mum, always one to take the initiative, found an elocution teacher to iron the broad Suffolk out of my accent. Prestwick was where I had the beginnings of primary education and I seemed to do well enough. Mum was delighted to discover that I was top of the class, but considerably less pleased a few months later when I appeared to have slipped to the bottom. When I had worked out that those at the front of the class, the children who were slower at their work, got out first at playtime, I slowed down until I found myself at the front of the class and first out to play!

In 1947 my little brother was born. Michael had a serious heart problem and it was years before the kind of surgery was done that might have saved his life. I have vivid memories of my baby brother. Crying made him turn dark blue, and I found that very frightening. In those days travelling shops used to go round Scottish towns and villages as most people didn't have cars. I remember one day being left holding Michael while Mum went out to one of the vans. He started to cry, and before long he was dark navy blue! I was absolutely terrified, convinced that he was going to die in my arms. Michael died aged four months, shortly after my seventh birthday.

A year later, when Dad secured a job in an Edinburgh hotel, we moved to that lovely city. Edinburgh is full of green places, and we lived beside one of the finest of them. The Meadows, which is just a fifteen-minute walk from the city centre, was the perfect place for a child. My playmate in the Meadows was a boy just my own age, my very first boyfriend! He and I were at school together, and my world fell apart when he announced that he was changing schools. Horrified, I ran home and pled with my mother to send me to his new school. My pleadings were successful, but I discovered later they were looking for a better school for me anyway. Imagine my broken heart when I arrived on my first day to discover that in my new school the girls were several miles away from the boys. Thus ended my first romance!

I had a special relationship with my father. Mum was the stronger of the two personalities by far, and I think my reaction to that was to be very protective of Dad, especially if there was any hint of disagreement between my parents. My father had never really recovered from his war experiences. One day he completely disappeared and we had no idea where he was. Life seemed to stand still through many long days. I remember the surge of relief when we heard that Dad had handed himself in at a police station somewhere south of the border. Not long afterwards he had a complete nervous breakdown and had to be admitted to hospital. When he was discharged we moved south to Leicester to be near his extended family. I had to leave school and all my friends, and I vividly remember sitting on the train as it left Edinburgh's Waverley Station feeling totally bereft. My life seemed to have fallen apart.

The Scottish and English school systems were different and I found myself a year behind my classmates. An educational psychologist decided that I was able, with extra tuition, to catch up. Perhaps the fear of going into a class with children a year younger than me inspired me to make an effort! Things had hardly had time to settle down when Dad had a heart attack and died at work. My great uncle met me at school and took me home to my mother, who said, 'Daddy has gone to be with Michael.' With those words, I felt the light go out in my life. I was just twelve years old. Almost immediately I asked Mum if we could go home to Edinburgh. When the news reached my old school that my father had died, the head of junior school wrote to Mum to say that if I wanted to go back to the school I would be eligible to apply to be a 'foundationer' and have my fees paid. To my delight we moved back and Mum found a job in telecommunications and bought a small flat in Newhaven, overlooking the River Forth.

It was wonderful being back with all my friends. Having caught up with my age group in the English school system I was now a year ahead of my contemporaries back in Scotland and I settled down into a comfortable existence of doing as little academic work as I could. A friend, who attended Scripture Union at school, invited me to go to an S.U. camp in the Christmas holidays. Although I don't remember much about that camp, it did, in a way, mark a new beginning. I wrote after camp, in a little copy of *Daily Light*, 'This day, January 7, 1954, I came under the gracious influence of the Holy Spirit. My purpose is fixed whether for life or death, to give my whole life to the Lord, seeing the Lord has redeemed me by his blood I trust he will never leave me.'

These are not the words of a twelve-year-old and I must have copied them from somewhere, yet I believe that when I wrote them I meant them. I had truly come under the gracious influence of the Holy Spirit. It was to be many years before I came to saving faith in the Lord Jesus Christ, but he never abandoned me. There was a long time when I turned my back on him, but his hand was always on me. Strangely, in my young mind, being a Christian and going to Bible College and being a missionary went together. You were one, so you did the other; maybe that was instilled into me at Scripture Union camp!

A student again

In 1975 Redcliffe College was an all women's institution, set right on the banks of the River Thames. Many hours were spent on the riverbank relaxing together, which sounds as though we didn't have enough work to do. Nothing could be further from the truth! But it was there in the golden sunshine of September that new students began to build relationships, some of which we knew would last a lifetime.

'How did you get into nursing?' I was asked several times in those early weeks.

How did I get into nursing? It certainly wasn't my first choice of career. I had wanted to be a doctor, but after moving back to Scotland I grew lazy and didn't get the grades I needed to pursue medicine. I did work hard in the drama club and had parts in several plays. One memorable part was Margaret in *Dear Brutus* in the Edinburgh Festival Fringe when I was thirteen or fourteen years old. The producer nearly sealed my fate when he took Mum aside and misquoted Noel Coward, 'Do put your daughter on the stage, Mrs Worthington. Do put your daughter on the stage.' Right away Mum could see my name in lights! She didn't know that I was in an agony of nerves every time in case I forgot my words.

Eventually I told Mum I wanted to be a nurse. 'You're not strong enough,' she replied. 'You couldn't walk the wards all day!' I didn't expect her to be thrilled at the idea, but it had never occurred to me she would object on health grounds. To her, nursing just couldn't compete with the Royal Shakespeare Company! Eventually I phoned our family doctor and explained my problem.'Is your mother there?' he asked. She was, and he told her that I was very healthy, and that if I were his daughter he would put me into the Western General Hospital School of Nursing. I don't suppose Mum was delighted, but she was flattered by the doctor's interest in me. So that's what happened and I was accepted to start in January 1960.

My first few months were spent in the male urology ward and from there I moved to radiotherapy. But I found it really hard to cope with children and young people dying of cancer. One wee boy affected me deeply; we just loved each other. He used to hang on the medicine trolley to get a whirl round the ward while I gave out the medicines. I was moved from that ward, but his parents asked me to go and see him just before he died. I went, and it nearly broke my heart to see him and his parents suffering. That experience raised all sorts of questions in my mind, not least, how a loving God could allow children to suffer.

By then I was attending Youth Fellowship in Newhaven Church and mixing with Christian young people, even going to prayer meetings. But at the same time I was at home in the nurses' social scene. I had started smoking and felt sophisticated holding a cigarette and a gin and tonic. That was when I began a balancing act between my two lives, my 'Christian' life with my church-going friends and my social life with my party-going friends. There being more days when we could party than go to church or prayer meetings, I did more partying than church-going.

While I was nursing I often worked nights. That wreaked havoc with my body clock and I took sleeping tablets to help me sleep during the day. My misuse of sleeping tablets continued for years and I found myself sometimes taking them when I was pressured because they made me feel better. Between smoking, drinking and taking sleeping pills I had embarked on an addictive lifestyle that gripped me, especially during times of stress, for many years. I was actually going out with a Christian at the time, and he thought I was a believer. The man who produced *Dear Brutus* was right, I could act!

I'm not sure that I was quite good enough at acting to persuade my nursing friends that I was a Christian, though I did go to the Nurses Christian Fellowship. Two of my colleagues who went, both senior to me, sometimes challenged me about my behaviour. Smoking was a real issue with them and once, after them talking to me, I screwed up all my cigarettes and flushed them down the toilet in an effort to be obedient to the Lord. One of these girls went abroad as a missionary and the other went on to Bible College in Glasgow. I look back at people like them who prayed faithfully for me over the years as the Lord keeping his hands on me after he first touched my heart when I was twelve. I certainly wasn't faithful to him, but he was to me.

After a year in neurosurgical nursing, I went down to London to do midwifery. Then, having completed the first part of my midwifery training, I moved north to Leicester to do part two. It was strange being back there after more than ten years, and stranger still some of the things we got up to. I lodged with a lady called Mrs Alsop who took in student midwives. She had no telephone, so when a woman went into labour her husband had to come and knock on my bedroom window and then I would go with him to his wife.

While we enjoyed worming out each other's life histories, Redcliffe students didn't just sit on the banks of the river chatting. The studies and disciplines of the College were no picnic. Yet my two years there prepared me in many ways for the tough times that awaited me thereafter.

2
Training and trials

My first few weeks at Redcliffe College were hard. To start with, I was suffering withdrawal from my nicotine addiction. I had smoked my last cigarette in a motorway service station en route to London. For years I had reached for a cigarette whenever I needed to relax; now I really did need to relax, but I could hardly smoke in a missionary training college! Of course, not being relaxed didn't help me sleep at nights, and sleep had been a problem at times of stress for years. At Redcliffe we shared rooms, which meant that I wasn't able to toss and turn, or put on the light and read until I felt sleepy, without disturbing my room-mates. That was a real trial for me throughout the whole two years.

Most of my fellow students were mature Christians and had a great deal of Bible knowledge, whereas I was really young in the faith. I had no doubt whatever that Christ died for me on the cross and that I was saved for time and eternity, but I didn't really know what it was to have a consistent day-by-day living relationship with him. Looking back I can see that with my addictive tendencies I would have struggled to live a Christian life in the secular world with all its temptations, whereas the Lord led me to Redcliffe where I would be nurtured and have the opportunity to grow within a Christian community for a whole two years. How gracious of him!

The staff were really supportive, especially the Principal, Miss Norah Vickers. At the start of our course she gave a series of talks in morning prayers on the work of the Holy Spirit. When she reached 'The Holy Spirit as Comforter' she said, 'If you've never been comforted by the Holy Spirit, you won't know what I'm talking about.' I clearly remember thinking, 'That's true; I don't know what you're talking about.' I prayed, 'God please help me to know the Holy Spirit as Comforter.' Not long after that I was given my first assignment; it was to go as part of a team with three other students to a women's group in nearby Kew to speak on the subject of the work of the Holy Spirit. I was asked to speak on the Holy Spirit as Comforter! As I didn't know anything about that in my own experience, I set about studying the subject as an academic exercise.

About that time something happened that hurt me very deeply. The details are now irrelevant, but my heart was broken. The day of my assignment was fast approaching and I just didn't have the heart for studying, but I had to get on with it. As I studied and worked out my talk, the Scriptures to which I was referred could have been written just for me. God knew exactly how hurt I was and ministered to me deep in my soul. It eventually dawned on me that he had answered my prayer to know the Holy Spirit as Comforter, but he couldn't do it without me first being really hurt and needing to be comforted. My talk was no longer dry and academic; I had experienced what I was talking about. How good God is and how perfect is his timing!

Practical work out in the community was an important feature of Redcliffe. For practical experience I was sent with a senior student to run a children's club. Audrey played the piano, which gave her a distinct advantage with the children. I didn't. Also she was a teacher and seemed to be relaxed in their presence. I certainly wasn't. My only experience of children was of very ill patients in hospital. Now, here I was surrounded by children and having to fight for their attention. I told them to sit down for a story and they ignored me. I was shocked. My student midwives had always done what they were told! The children ran circles round me and I simply didn't know how to control them. If I'm honest, I have to admit to actually disliking them. Some trainee missionary! Eventually I learned to play the guitar, which helped a little.

From that abortive attempt at children's work I was sent to a youth club in London. This was for teenagers and, as I left after my first night, I wondered why they bothered to come. It was meant to be a Bible club, but the youngsters were not in the least interested. They just wouldn't do anything they were told, far less listen to the Bible being read or taught! One week, when I was ill, Miss Vickers went in my place and it was such a relief to hear what happened in my absence. The young folk were as badly behaved for her as they had been for me, and when Miss Vickers told one girl to sit down, she flatly refused. So the Principal led her by the arm to a chair. The girl rushed out of the hall only to return with a policeman, claiming that she had been assaulted! At least Miss Vickers' experience showed me that the problem wasn't entirely mine.

While at Redcliffe I was encouraged to choose a life verse. I chose Philippians 3:10, 11:'I want to know Christ and the power of his resurrection and the fellowship of sharing in his sufferings, becoming like him in his death, and so, somehow, to attain to the resurrection from the dead.' Having wasted many years, I now had a great desire to know Christ, to really know him, not just about him. I often prayed,'God, please help me to know Christ and make me more like him.' That was another prayer God answered, and has gone on answering, and will go on answering until I go to heaven. I was quite naïve and had no idea what a painful process becoming even the slightest little bit more Christ-like would be. More and more things in my life were exposed that were far from Christ-like and had to be dealt with; things that would hinder God using me in his service.

My verse

The programme at Redcliffe, as well as encouraging daily devotions, included regular 'quiet days'. These were days of prayer and fasting, and we usually had someone from outside the College to lead us in several meditations during the day. Towards the end of my time there an Anglican Canon led us through one such quiet day.

'I asked the Lord to give me a Scripture verse for each one of you,' he told us. 'Miss Vickers gave me a list of your names, and I have written beside each name the verse I believe the Lord has given me for you. During the course of the day I will call each of you into my room and give you your verse.' When I was called in, the Scripture verse I was given was 1 Thessalonians 2:7-8. 'We were gentle among you, like a mother caring for her little children. We loved you so much that we were delighted to share with you not only the gospel of God but our lives as well, because you had become so dear to us.'

'This is for you,' the Canon said, 'because the ministry I believe God is saying you will have is a caring one, where your care isn't just a job. You will share your life with those you are caring for, just as in a family where the mother cares for her children.' When I was given my Scripture verse I dutifully highlighted it in my Bible, but I really didn't think it was the right verse for me and put it out of my mind. With my track record with children I didn't feel it was likely that the Lord was planning that I spend my missionary career mothering children who would be so dear to me that we became a family! I was a midwife; after all, I helped bring babies into the world and then left them to be brought up in their own families!

By the time I completed my second year at Redcliffe I had been accepted to work with the Africa Inland

Mission. Because I had only been a Christian for two years the Mission wanted me to do a year of pastoral work in my own congregation in Edinburgh. The minister, Rev. Alec Aitken, was not at all sure what to do with me. Eventually he suggested I should run a Vacation Bible School … for children! Not wanting to refuse the very first thing that had been requested of me, I agreed weakly. Thankfully, I had a willing band of twelve helpers from the congregation which made the whole thing possible, and even enjoyable. The Vacation Bible School showed the need for a week-night club for children who didn't attend Sunday School. It was then that I discovered that Edinburgh children were no different from those in London. They too ran rings round me! I was glad to be going back to the safety and security of nursing and midwifery at the end of my year in Edinburgh!

Rev. Alec Aitken

My first contact with Georgie was when, after finishing her course at Redcliffe Missionary Training College, she was sent by A.I.M. to do a year's practical work with me in the parish of Newhaven in Edinburgh. She arrived to start her appointment just prior to my leaving with my family for our month's holiday. I vividly remember asking her if she could cope with a summer children's club. She did protest that she was never good at working with children, but despite her own feelings of inadequacy for such work she took up the challenge and, with the help of some of the women in the church, ran a successful children's club which subsequently developed into a weekly Thursday night club with considerable success. During that year she worked diligently in the work of the congregation, helping with the heavy load of visiting to the hospital and to the many elderly. She was an enormous help and endeared herself to the congregation. Over that period she became a very close friend to us all in a friendship that has lasted to this day.

Many of my friends at Redcliffe knew, by the end of their time at college, to which country the Lord wanted them to go. I didn't. Although I had been in Kenya I didn't have a sense of calling to go back there. A.I.M. had a need for a nurse midwife in Kagando Hospital in Western Uganda and I was asked to prayerfully consider if the Lord would have me go there. God spoke to me through the story in Joshua 3, where the priests were to carry the Ark of the Covenant across the River Jordan. The river was in flood and it presented a huge obstacle to their crossing to the Promised Land. It wasn't until the priests put their feet into the water that the waters of the Jordan parted and they were able to carry the Ark safely across on dry land. God showed me that I too must take a step of faith and see if the way opened up for me to go to Uganda. I declared my willingness to go if God opened the way.

My barrier wasn't a river but provision of finance. At that time A.I.M. held to the faith principle of never mentioning financial needs. Provision of finance was considered God's seal that the missionary was going to the place of his choosing. I set out on a tour of deputation around churches and A.I.M. prayer groups, being introduced and letting people get to know me. I asked for prayer as I headed to Uganda. The date for my valedictory service at Newhaven Church was set and

I waited, knowing the service wouldn't go ahead until at least 80 per cent of my required financial support came in. How can God supply money if you can't tell people that you need the money? I cried to the Lord and in my devotions he gave me Jeremiah 33:3 (av), 'Call unto me, and I will answer thee, and show thee great and mighty things, which thou knowest not.'

Things really moved fast after that. I was in Darlington visiting my mother, who had by then remarried, and my stepfather, a very dear and gracious man. One evening they had guests for dinner, Doctor Marvin and Louise Compher. Marvin, a minister from Tampa in Florida, was on an exchange with the minister of Northgate United Reformed Church in Darlington. I was introduced as a missionary going to Uganda. Marvin, without hesitation, asked, 'How is your support coming along?' I got such a shock I nearly fell off the chair! He was the first person who had openly asked me about support. Not only that, he said he knew his church in Tampa had a balance in its missionary fund. The American overlapped by a week with the minister of Northgate Church, and before leaving to go back to Tampa he asked the minister to suggest that the people of Northgate covenant towards my support. When Newhaven Church, which had already committed to support me, was joined by several other churches and individuals, everyone's reaction was, 'Why didn't you tell us you needed support?' And in my heart I thought, 'Because then I wouldn't have known that it was God himself who prompted his people to promise the money.'

The way to Uganda had opened. My valedictory

service went ahead and it was wonderful. Maurice Wheatley, the Home Director of A.I.M., was there with many representatives from the Scottish A.I.M. prayer groups and others from Darlington. I was prayed for and officially sent out as the first missionary from Newhaven Church of Scotland. My heart was full of praise to God and of confidence that I was going to the place of his choosing, to help to take the gospel to Africa. I drove down to London and stayed at Redcliffe College overnight and then was seen off at Heathrow by Miss Vickers and other friends. My car was to be shipped to Uganda via Mombasa and I flew to Entebbe, full of excitement at going to serve the Lord in the hospital at Kagando. I was about to come down to earth with a very big bump!

By the time I arrived in Kampala I had a high fever and an infection that laid me low. I had to stay there, along with the missionaries who had come to collect me, until I was well enough to travel to Kagando. Uganda, at that time, was in a state of political turmoil that had erupted into war. Idi Amin had overseen the slaughter of rebellious tribes and expelled all non-Ugandan citizens, including upwards of 60,000 Asians. In 1978, just as I arrived in the country, and in response to Ugandan aggression, Tanzanian invaders advanced through southern Uganda. Eventually we arrived at Kagando Hospital and I was shown a dear wee house that was to be mine. Then I was introduced to the world of water drums, paraffin fridges, pressure lamps and gas cylinders. Although we were living in a country at war, our only news of the situation came to us via BBC World Service.

I had been sent out as a missionary of the Lord Jesus Christ to the people of Uganda, but when I arrived I couldn't even say 'hello', let alone tell them about Jesus. Amazing as it might seem, I was totally unprepared for the inability to communicate. I knew I would have to learn the language, but the actual practicalities of being unable to say a word had never really dawned on me. It hit me forcibly when, just after my arrival, a man was admitted with an intestinal obstruction. As there was no one to operate, the man died and I couldn't even tell him that Jesus loved him.

Very soon the situation around us became more and more difficult, and not only because of the war. There was a serious outbreak of cholera in the Kagando area and cholera is one of the most rapidly fatal illnesses known. Vast amounts of intravenous fluids were needed to treat the patients that flocked to the hospital and we hadn't anything like enough, and no electricity for distilling more. Thankfully it was the rainy season and rainwater could be filtered and given intravenously. I was so stressed that I started doubting my clinical judgement. For example, if I used precious intravenous fluids on someone who didn't survive, I then tortured myself because someone else was dying who might have survived had I still had that intravenous fluid to give him. Strange as it may seem, after all my years in maternity units it was in Kagando hospital that I saw my first maternal death. I found that really hard.

Looking back, with the benefit of both hindsight and maturity, I can see that the situation in Kagando, and in all of Uganda, was truly awful. But at the time

I felt that I was a complete failure. Having been built up by the thought of being a missionary, here I was, within a matter of weeks, a physical and emotional wreck. Not only that, but I resorted to my old coping strategy of taking sleeping tablets to dull the pain of it all. My poor fellow missionaries, who were already under a huge amount of strain, found me an even bigger load to bear. They tried to get word to A.I.M. that I was in trouble but all communications were down. Eventually the cholera subsided and we were able to get enough petrol to take me to Kampala, and from there to Nairobi. I was sure that my next stop would be Scotland, that I would be returned straight home as a failure.

Battered and bruised

Dr Dick Anderson, the A.I.M. International General Secretary, was in Nairobi to meet me. 'Please don't send me home,' I begged, as we settled down for a serious discussion. 'I'm the first missionary my congregation has ever sent out and I don't want to let them down. I can't go back as a failure.' After we talked and prayed, Dr Dick had a suggestion. 'Your car has been shipped to Mombasa. I think you should go down and see if you can clear it. Get the car then spend a while with the Lavers. Pa and Pearl Lavers have a counselling and healing ministry.' I never knew Pa Lavers' Christian name. He was the first headmaster of St Andrews, a famous boarding school at Turi, and was always affectionately known as Pa, even in retirement.

As I relaxed in their loving home under the healing ministry, Pa and Pearl were a real comfort and strength to me. They prayed with me day after day and helped me work through all the traumas of Uganda. That dear couple were God's 'comfort blankets' for my broken and bruised heart, mind and body. But although they helped me tremendously it would be a long time before I would grasp the reality of the verse, 'For we know that our old self is crucified with him so that the body of sin might be done away with, that we should no longer be slaves to sin' (Rom. 6:6). Every time I read that verse I would argue, 'That's my whole problem; my old self isn't crucified. Why else would I always react to stress in the wrong way?' What I was in fact saying was that God's Word isn't true. One day, years later, it came to me that it isn't how I see myself that matters, it is how God sees me – and he sees me from the vantage point of eternity. God sees me, my sinful self, with Jesus on the cross, crucified, dead and buried! I no longer have to react to my old self or be bound by it. My old self *is* crucified! I may not always feel it gone, but I can count on the truth. That is how God sees it and I can claim that fact in times of stress, of which there would be many in the years to come.

Just before I went to the Lavers I spent some days in an Anglican guesthouse where I met Lorna Eglin and Betty Allcock, two South African missionaries who were working in Kajiado, in Kenya. They had recently started a Child Care Centre for the rehabilitation of children with physical disabilities. Lorna and Betty had asked A.I.M. for a nurse to come and help them, but had been refused on the grounds that the Mission should not start a medical work in Kajiado, as there was a already a district hospital there.

'Why don't you come and spend a few weeks with us?' they asked, when they realised I was a stray nurse just out of Uganda with nowhere to go. As I looked at these two earnest ladies, the thought went through my head, 'If you only knew what a failure I am, you certainly wouldn't want me at Kajiado.'

3
To Kajiado

It was on 1 April 1979, having spent several weeks in the tender and loving care of Pa and Pearl Lavers, that I arrived at Kajiado to meet up with Lorna and Betty again. Dr Dick Anderson took me there and what a welcome we received. It was obvious that I couldn't return to Uganda and, as Lorna and Betty had already put in a request for me to join them in their work, at least temporarily, they were very excited when I arrived. When Dr Dick wisely told me to tell them all about Uganda, it was not easy to begin that story. Despite all the counselling I had received from the Lavers, I still feared being sent back home to Scotland. I would have done anything, even clean toilets, rather than leave Africa as a failure. These mature missionaries listened, not judgmentally but kindly, and at the end of my story they hugged me and from then on made it their ministry to rebuild my shattered self-confidence. Then they told me their story.

Lorna had started a boarding school for Maasai girls away back in 1959, and Betty joined her nine years later. Lorna's Maasai name was *Ng'oto Ntoyie*, 'Mother of the Girls'. She and Betty were eager, after all these years, to leave the schoolwork to others and get out to the Maasai villages. At last, when there was a Maasai headmistress available to take over, they were free. As they travelled around sharing the gospel in the Maasai villages, they realised that providing literacy classes for women and older girls would give them regular contact. They were planning for the first course when suddenly the whole venture took an unexpected turn – the senior chief and other tribal elders insisted they teach the Maasai warriors instead! Lorna and Betty had some wonderful times when teaching the young men to read, men just leaving their warriorhood and becoming junior elders. But it was when two Maasai men became Christians, and wanted to go out witnessing in the villages with the ladies, that their ministry changed direction because it soon became apparent that the men needed to study the Bible to better understand the basics of their faith. The class, which started with two students, soon had a dozen and the Kajiado Evangelists Training Centre was developed where any Maasai men who wanted to know more of the Word could come for two weeks of Bible teaching each month. They spent the other two weeks going round the villages teaching the people what they had learnt. Over the months the number attending grew to fifty, and would have grown further had there not been limited sleeping space. It was these men who gave Betty her Maasai name *Kokoo oo Imuran*, 'Grandmother of the Warriors'.

While Lorna and Betty were involved with the Evangelists Training Programme, famine struck and they started taking milk powder and maize meal out to the villages to those families who needed help. Finding that some of the toddlers, whose mothers had new babies breast-feeding, were desperately undernourished and needed special care, the missionaries hastily converted a partially constructed building into a baby house. Two big beds were made for the toddlers to sleep on and house-mothers were hired to love and feed these little ones. When the children grew stronger they were able to return home. Another need became apparent as the two women went around Maasai villages, the need of help for disabled children. When one frustrated granny came to their house desperate about her little disabled grandson, Kumoin, Lorna took a step of faith and promised her that when he was old enough to start school there would be a place for him to be cared for and to receive the treatment he needed.

Some months later a pastor from the United States, who had helped them during a previous famine, told the missionaries that there was a group in Canada who wanted to donate a regular monthly amount of money to help needy Maasai children. Lorna and Betty rejoiced, seeing that as God's provision of funding for a place for disabled children. But they still needed a building. The very same day that they heard about this gift from Canada, the two of them were due to visit friends in Nairobi. Winifred Robinson and Rosemary Sandercock were British nurses working with the Flying Doctor Service and Lorna and Betty had often worked closely with them. Robbie and Rosemary took advantage of the crowds who gathered in remote villages to receive aid and listen to the gospel to do medical and immunisation clinics. As the four women sat down for lunch, Lorna and Betty told them of their good news and their friends excitedly added more good news – they too had received a special gift. Being the International Year of the Child, a Nairobi firm had given them a substantial sum of money to be used for children's work.

It was joyfully agreed that the money would be used to put up a little building, a short-stay home where children with various medical problems could be cared for while help was being sought. Robbie and Rosemary needed a 'holding ground' for the children they found in their clinics who were in need of surgery. It often happened that by the time they had found a charity bed in a Nairobi hospital, and a surgeon who was willing to donate his services, they had lost track of the child in need of surgery because the Maasai are semi-nomadic and follow the rains and available grazing for their cattle. The famine over, Lorna and Betty no longer had the place that had been used for undernourished toddlers needing special care. The disabled children they had found were on their minds, as was their promise to that granny that there would soon be a place for children like Kumoin.

Very quickly a Committee was formed, a plot chosen on the Africa Inland Church (A.I.C.) compound and the building of the Kajiado Child Care Centre was started. On 1 January 1979 the Centre was dedicated and the first children admitted to *Enkaji oo Nkera*, the House of Children. Three Maasai house-mothers were employed to care for the children, who were mostly disabled following polio. Some, who had tuberculosis, needed daily injections of streptomycin at Kajiado District Hospital; others had skin problems or were blind or partially sighted. Lorna and Betty were quite overwhelmed and needed help.

One day they took the children with eye problems to the Christophel Blindenmission (C.B.M.) Eye Unit at Presbyterian Church of East Africa (P.C.E.A.) Kikuyu Hospital on the outskirts of Nairobi. The German sister in charge asked them where the children were from, and when they explained about the recently opened Child Care Centre she exclaimed, 'My brother is looking for children like those in your Centre! C.B.M. has just agreed to start helping children with other disabilities, not just those with visual handicaps.' Before they left the hospital she gave them directions to her brother's house in Nairobi. While the children, to their great delight, were fed juice and biscuits, Mr Opitz gave Lorna and Betty advice and help in filling in application forms for funding from C.B.M. 'You need to apply for a Land Rover, money for salaries for house-mothers, running costs and money to build accommodation for the nurse you will need,' he told them. I can still remember the thrill in my heart as they told their story, and I wondered if I might possibly be that nurse. I knew they were praying about it, and the children were so adorable that I just loved them to bits, but I was still raw from my time in Uganda and hardly dared to hope that I might be able to stay in Kajiado.

The whole question of working in Kenya was academic anyway, because when I left Uganda I entered Kenya on a visitor's pass, and it was endorsed to say that I could not apply for a work permit while on that pass. We all prayed that if the Lord wanted me to stay at Kajiado and work in the Child Care Centre, he would overrule that endorsement and I would be granted a work permit without first having to leave Kenya. I had already been booked on a three-month Swahili language course in Nairobi, and when it ended an application was made for a work permit. It was granted with no questions asked by the Immigration Department and I was assigned by the A.I.C. Staffing Board to work at Kajiado. I was absolutely thrilled! That is how a midwife tutor with no orthopaedic experience – and who disliked children's work! – came to be superintendent of a home for physically disabled children. Who but God would ever have planned that? Not me, for sure! Yet how many times over the years have I thought that the work couldn't have fitted me better, or given me more joy.

I arrived at Kajiado with a very firm grasp of my own weakness, to work with a small group of disabled children and uneducated village women. Nobody could ever have guessed what God would do in and through that little band of people with all our weaknesses, both seen and unseen. Many times in the years that followed I would prove God true to his word: 'My grace is sufficient for you, for my power is made perfect in weakness' (2 Cor. 12:9).

First Impressions

My first impressions of the Child Care Centre were of fun, laughter and singing – but no tears! Eighteen children with varying degrees of mobility rushed at me whenever I appeared, waiting with heads bowed saying *ng'asak*, 'greet me!' Maasai children always take the initiative in greeting and wait patiently until a hand is laid on each head. There were plaster casts with holes worn in knees and heels from too much crawling on the concrete paths. Then there were the runny noses! I had never in all my life seen so much *olkuluk*; invariably I would find a stain where a toddler had hugged me around my knees and buried a snotty nose lovingly in my skirt! Being used to just wearing one little cloth which is seldom washed, the children wore sweaters that were turned back to front when soiled and then inside out, and only put in the wash when all four sides were dirty.

It was fun in the dormitories watching as their wee bare black bottoms slithered across brightly coloured floor tiles en route to the shower. And that was followed by squeals of delight as water sprayed down from the ceiling, washing off the Lifebuoy soapsuds – medicated as a token gesture to control the secondary infections of ringworm and scabies, and negated by the use of one towel for all! Toddlers were wrapped individually in sheets and put down to sleep, all cuddled up together on one big bed just as they would sleep at home on one cow-skin.

Songs echoed constantly around the compound as the children pedalled furiously on exercise bicycles in the grass-roofed playhouse, under the supervision of

Agnes, the nursery school teacher.

> *Little children, God loves you*
> *with a love that doesn't pass away*
> *like the seasons.*

That song went on forever, over and over, starting each successive verse with the name of another child!

Each member of the team brought her own individual gifts. Rebecca was the born leader, motivating everyone with her enthusiasm and love for her Lord. From a distant tribe – the Samburu – and despised by her witchdoctor husband because she bore him no children, she ran away home to her people in the north of Kenya when his cruelty became too much for her. A missionary there called *Naado*, the tall one, led her to the Lord. In generous sympathy, Rebecca's sister promised to give her the next child she bore. True to her word, a son was born and put into Rebecca's empty arms. The new 'mother' called her son

Samuel, and from then on, in keeping with Maasai tradition, she was known as Mother of Samuel, *Ng'oto Samuel*. After a while the missionary reminded Rebecca that she belonged to her husband, he had paid the dowry, and that she should return to him.

On her way home with her baby, Ng'oto Samuel passed through Kajiado and went

Ng'oto Samuel with one of the children.

to church there. When Lorna and Betty saw her they were impressed by her obvious love for the Lord, yet puzzled because she still wore her Maasai traditional dress. They invited her in for tea to hear her story. That was the beginning of a long relationship as Ng'oto Samuel helped Lorna and Betty with village evangelism and taught Samburu Christian songs sung to traditional tunes. Previously they only knew Maasai versions of our English hymns. She also showed the village women that they didn't need to wait for a dress to wear in church; they were welcome to come in their traditional cloths and beads. Ng'oto Samuel had been one of the housemothers in the original baby house, and now was senior housemother in the Child Care Centre. She gave me my Maasai name 'Naado', carefully chosen in honour of the missionary who had led her to the Lord in Samburu. It was also fitting because I was taller than Lorna and Betty. I was very proud to be given a Maasai name and appreciated the sense of belonging that came with it. Ng'oto Samuel was single-minded in her service for the Lord; her whole life spoke of Christ.

Lorna and Betty had seen a wee boy at the district hospital suffering from the effects of polio and they arranged for him to be brought to the Child Care Centre on discharge. But when they went back to enquire about him they found that he had been sent home. That gave me my first of many journeys out on to the plains to follow up disabled children. After many enquiries about Ntuyoto's whereabouts I eventually arrived at his home and found the boy crawling in the cow dung, covered in dust and scabies. He was pulling himself along by his arms and dragging thin, floppy, spidery legs behind him. Ntuyoto's father walked the many rough miles to the Child Care Centre to see if it were a fit place for his son before giving permission for him to be admitted. Soon Ntuyoto was fitted with

calipers to keep his weak legs straight and over a long time, and with a huge amount of effort, he learned to walk with crutches. When the great day came and he took his first steps alone, I heard him muttering something. It was *Ashe Yesu*, 'thank you, Jesus!' Ng'oto Samuel had been praying with him every night that Jesus would help him to walk.

Children wearing "Thank you Jesus" tee shirts.

My heart sank whenever I saw Ng'oto Samuel's old witchdoctor husband hobbling up the road towards us. He was recognisable from afar because one leg was much shorter than the other. An Oloiboni traditionally has no land of his own, and has to be given a place to stay, but he was so quarrelsome that he often had to move. When that happened he would come to me for help in moving him and all his gourds, bones, powders and potions, to another village. Was this really what a missionary should be doing? But with Ng'oto Samuel's faithful witness he eventually came to the Lord. When that miracle happened we missionaries and the local evangelists had a great ceremony and burial service as Ng'oto Samuel helped him pour out all the potions from the little gourds into a crater-shaped 'grave' of cow dung. The gourds were scattered in the cattle enclosure so that they would be trampled by the cows when they came home. The other two housemothers were Martha and Ninana. Martha spent all her 'free' time going round the Maasai villages preaching, and when she wasn't preaching she sang at the top of her voice. She never missed an opportunity to testify to the love of God. Ninana, one of her arms paralysed, cooked vast and endless pots of food on the specially built low gas stove.

When Lorna and Betty were not teaching the evangelists, going out preaching in the villages or doing famine relief work, they enjoyed being involved with the children. Betty was usually either seated at her typewriter communicating with prayer supporters and donors, or at her sewing machine making or mending clothes for the children or making sheets and curtains for the dormitories. She kept the money straight too. Lorna was handyman extraordinaire, designing all the buildings for the Child Care Centre and supervising plumbing and carpentry. Cooking and baking were also among her areas of expertise. When unexpected visitors came, as they very often did, Lorna concocted meals from what was available while Betty told them the story of the Child Care Centre. Lorna was fluent in the language and it was she who wrote the Maasai grammar book that I spent long hours studying.

I also spent many hours pouring over Professor Huxted's book *Poliomyelitis,* which was written as a textbook for a rehabilitation centre in Uganda. It contained instructions on how to make basic calipers and crutches and gave simple techniques for making plaster casts and splints. A visiting physiotherapist taught me the basics of stretching tendons shortened by polio, and I continued learning, only slightly comforted by the knowledge that I couldn't do quite so much harm not knowing what I was doing helping disabled children to walk as I would have done not knowing what I was doing delivering babies!

Taking the wheel

The driving was exciting and challenging! I just loved the off-road driving, although the roads were almost as demanding. If a father wanted his disabled child collected from a village, he needed to make a path for the car to pass, which involved cutting down bushes and notching trees to mark the way. Often a warrior wearing a red cloth knotted over each shoulder ran, cloth flying in the breeze, in front of the car pointing out all the holes or stumps that could be a danger. They frequently forgot that a car is wider than a person and landed us in trouble. Many of these early paths were repeatedly used by other vehicles and became quite big 'roads' over the years. I derived huge satisfaction at the thought that we had 'made' these roads! Sometimes whoever was guiding me in the car said, 'Follow that path there', and I, seeing only grass and bush, asked, 'What path where?' 'That little "path for people" over there!' the exasperated reply would come back. Maasai always walk in a line, one behind the other, in case the leader surprises a snake. These little paths twisted and turned through the grass. All I could do was to try to keep the front wheels on either side of the little 'path for people' and hope for the best.

When the children had to be taken to hospital in Nairobi, which was quite a frequent occurrence, we always drove back home through Nairobi Game Park. This was great light relief after what usually was a stressful day. It was there I discovered that the Maasai are much more frightened of buffalo than of lion. And on these trips I learned that I needed to react very quickly to the words *enkulak* and *enkik*, and hoped there would be a suitably safe place to stop for the child to 'go' behind a bush!

Finding surgical help for the children in these early days was difficult. Occasionally a Flying Doctor surgeon operated at Kajiado Hospital and then the child was discharged to the Child Care Centre straight after surgery. One day we heard of a doctor at the Magadi Soda Company's private hospital, who had orthopaedic experience. I arranged to take a boy who had bilateral talipes – clubfeet – hopefully for him to have surgery. The boy was about twelve years old and had learnt to walk on the outside edges of his feet thus causing his soles to face each other. The four-hour drive from Kajiado was magnificent, first across the wide-open Maasai plains to the outskirts of Nairobi and then the glorious long drive down, about 4,000 feet, to Lake Magadi, the southernmost soda lake in the Kenyan Rift Valley. The soda, which is one of Kenya's main exports, is 'harvested' by huge machinery on the thick crust of soda. Lorries drive over this crust to take the soda to the railway. Soda is mostly used as fertiliser, but, surprisingly, also in the manufacturing of motor tyres! The lake produces salt too, and when the salty water crystallises and is swept into piles it turns a beautiful pink colour and makes a memorable scene.

As we drove down, the lake looked bigger and bigger and the pink patches more and more striking, until we eventually arrived at the causeway that took us across to Magadi town and the Magadi Soda Company. At less than 2,000 feet above sea level the heat was oppressive. I almost envied the boy I had brought to the hospital for he was washed and put into a nice clean bed with a ceiling fan over him while I, sweating and covered with dust, set off on the long climb back up to 6,000 feet with the only good view being in the rear-view mirror. The surgeon managed to straighten Parloshi's feet by fusing the ankle joints and pinning his feet in position. I made that trip many times with different children and always enjoyed it, especially on the outward journey.

Our early need for boots and calipers for the children who had polio was met by the Association for the Physically Disabled of Kenya (A.P.D.K.) mobile clinic. They came each month, measured the children, and the next month brought back their boots and calipers. As the number of children increased, this wait became frustrating and I started taking the children to the A.P.D.K. Clinic in Nairobi. Another option was the orthopaedic workshop of the Kenyatta National Hospital, but the wait there was so long that the children had grown out of the calipers by the time they received them! There was also an expensive shop in Nairobi where, for a couple of years, there was a well-trained technician. I bought my plaster shears there, my very first piece of orthopaedic equipment!

Meanwhile, the Child Care Centre was growing. By January 1980, sixteen children had finished nursery and started 'big school'. I was so proud of them as they all set off for their very first day at real school, the boys in their royal blue shorts and blue and white checked shirts and the girls in their pale green blouses and dark green tunics, the uniform chosen by Lorna in 1959 and which remains today. I discovered afterwards that the children were really quite naughty. What other family has eight children starting together in one class? Our kids were confident in each other's company and not nearly as overawed as the other little primary school Standard One children. To make matters worse, the teachers, not used to dealing with children with disabilities, were frightened to discipline them, so they got off with a great deal of mischief.

The schools our children attended daily were mostly boarding schools and the boys and girls went home for the holidays. Our children went home for the school holidays too, in April, August and December, unless they were undergoing treatment which couldn't be carried on at home. One wee boy, Manja, was allergic to sunlight. His skin was scarred from the effects of the sun and he was almost blind. He often had huge ulcers on the tip of his nose and lips and had to have them cleaned twice daily. Manja wasn't clever at school either and had to repeat Standard One three times in the unit for the visually handicapped. But while we tend to look on the outward appearance God looks at the heart and Manja, in his own simple way, trusted the

Lord. Just before one school holiday Manja asked to go home even though he needed daily treatment. He hadn't been home for eighteen months and we had lost contact with his mother. Manja's treatment was complicated and without it his skin would break down and be covered in running sores again. I explained to him that I didn't dare let him go home without some contact with his mother, but he didn't grasp my meaning. When the vehicle came to take the children to his area, he was standing clutching his little paper bag of possessions waiting to go with them. I stopped him and his heart broke.

Later I heard Ng'oto Samuel talking to him in the kitchen, 'Manja, you know Jesus, don't you?'

'Yes I know him,' replied Manja through his tears.

'Well, go into the playhouse by yourself and ask Jesus to tell your mother to come.'

As I walked over to my house for lunch I heard Manja pouring out his heart to Jesus. I was in tears too as I pleaded with the Lord to answer that wee boy's prayer. Two days later a man arrived at the Child Care Centre and said that Manja's mother had asked him to come and see if she could have her son home for the holidays! He was prepared to escort the boy the 150 miles to his home and take the necessary medicines. As Manja headed off in the direction of the bus stop, Ng'oto Samuel shouted after him, 'Remember to say thank you to Jesus! He heard your prayer!'

How lovely it was to see God revealing himself to these little ones and to see them coming to trust in the Saviour for themselves!

PRAYER LETTER – KAJIADO JULY 1979

Dear Friends,
In my last letter I asked you to pray that the Lord would lead me to the place of his choosing. He has done just that. It is a newly opened Child Care Centre for Maasai children who need long-term medical treatment. At the moment there are twenty-seven children, seventeen of whom have undergone surgery to correct deformities caused by polio. It is thrilling to care for these wee ones and gradually teach them to walk with the aid of calipers and crutches.

Having fun on the swing

Then there is no stopping them – sometimes my heart is in my mouth as I see a child with a leg in plaster or caliper, hurtling down the slide or swinging high on the swings. The children called me 'Naado' (Maasai for Tall One) but they must have decided that wasn't respectful enough because now it's 'Mrs Naado'!

Living with the children are four Mamas – the chief one being Ng'oto Samuel. She is a living testimony to the love of the Lord Jesus Christ.

We praise the Lord for funds to complete the building which will include accommodation for forty children, dormitories for those attending school and a wee flat for me. We also praise the Lord for the openings the work gives for spreading the Word of God in villages.

With love
Yours aye,
Georgie

4
On a wing and a prayer

Although at first I found the whole subject of personalised financial support difficult, I came to really appreciate the sense of being one of a team – a number of people, individuals and groups, giving financially in order that I could be on the mission field, backed up by those who were committed to praying for me and for the work. While many prayed faithfully that God would supply our needs, who could ever have guessed how he would answer them! The team was about to get very much bigger.

One day a knock came to the door. It was, to my great surprise, the Air Adviser to the British High Commission in Nairobi, to ask if we would like to be adopted by an R.A.F. squadron! He explained that the United Kingdom Mobile Air Movements Squadron (U.K.M.A.M.S.) had been giving help to a children's home in Kathmandu. But as they were no longer flying there, they were looking for a similar establishment in Kenya that would benefit from their help. He explained that, if we agreed to being adopted, anything that my friends could get to R.A.F. Lyneham in Wiltshire would be flown out to us free of charge whenever there was space on a flight coming to Kenya. Agreed! We didn't hesitate for a second! Little did we know what a huge help that would be. For many years the Air Adviser in the British High Commission in Nairobi would liaise with the Wing Commander of U.K.M.A.M.S. to keep the whole operation going to our best advantage. It was as if the children had a whole squadron of doting adopted uncles and even a few aunts! Nothing was too much trouble, and their concern for us was very evident. Many remain friends to this day.

My mother was in her element as she longed to be practically involved in the work of the Child Care Centre. She set about collecting clothes and shoes and soon had a whole garage full, literally! Friends in Darlington then drove the huge boxes down to the Lyneham air base. This was repeated all over the country as supporters collected whatever they thought would be useful. Soon the children in the Centre were the best dressed in Kenya! The Nuffield Orthopaedic Centre in Oxford and other hospitals sent us special 'Pedro' orthopaedic boots which their young patients had outgrown, as well as crutches and sticks, walking frames and wheelchairs. Hospitals also donated medicines and bandages and tons and tons of out-of-date plaster bandages that were still being used when I left Kajiado sixteen years later.

Plaster bandage is expensive and I don't remember ever buying a single roll. God was very gracious to me because I was a real novice in applying plaster casts and often had to remake splints because I didn't made a good enough job of them first time round. Imagine how I would have felt if each roll of plaster bandage had cost a lot of money.

The Association with U.K.M.A.M.S. allowed for personal involvement in the Child Care Centre in a really lovely way. The seven-year-old son of a family I knew in Aberdeen entered a competition run by his local newspaper. Entrants had to write what they would do if they were given £10. Andrew wrote to the newspaper saying, 'My friend Georgie works with wee disabled Maasai children in Kenya. If I had £10 I would buy a small tricycle so that her children would have fun doing their exercises.' Andrew won the competition. The tricycle was bought and flown out to us accompanied by a second tricycle given by a little girl who had just graduated to a bicycle and wanted to give her old tricycle to the Kenyan children.

A very real relationship was built up over the time of our involvement with U.K.M.A.M.S.. When R.A.F. personnel re-enter the U.K. at R.A.F. Lyneham they put their local currency coins in a charity jar, from which outgoing staff buy coins to take with them. The profit from that bought a welder and a cement mixer, and even rowing machines and exercise bicycles which we would otherwise never have been able to afford. Members of the squadron came to visit us whenever they were in Kenya and even helped complete a building project at a local primary school. Other things were, however, much more exciting to the children. At one point we had two tons of sweets and huge boxes of biscuits filling our garage! They were en route to Ethiopia when the planned transport failed. On another occasion the Chairman of Edinburgh's Heart of Midlothian Football Club heard that our youngsters loved football but only had socks tied into a huge knot for a ball and he arranged for a number of match footballs to be sent out. The boys were thrilled. When they arrived we established the Heart of Midlothian Kajiado Reserve Football Team!

Every year the Aero Club of East Africa has an air show and, for several years, the children were invited as guests of honour. Our friends in the British High Commission arranged transport and packed lunches from a hotel in Nairobi, and the children were driven to the air show, visiting Daphne Sheldrick's sanctuary for baby elephants and rhinos en route. They were very excited to see a tiny baby elephant with sun-burnt ears, whose mother had been killed by poachers, leaving her baby with no shade. There was even more excitement at the air show – 'men with smoke pouring out of their legs, falling from the sky', otherwise the Red Devils parachute team. One year the children were even given joyrides in an aeroplane. I didn't join them for that because I hate flying and the concept of JOY in a plane made no sense to me whatsoever!

Rescuers and helpers

One day the Royal Engineers came to my rescue, quite literally. I had had a blow-out when driving my car back from Mombasa and, because the vehicle somersaulted three times, it was in no fit state for taking children to hospital a week later and I was forced to use Lorna and Betty's Land Cruiser instead. Having delivered the children, I set off on my own back to Kajiado. Suddenly a cyclist pulled out in front of me. I slammed my foot on the brake, the Land Cruiser spun round on the wet road, and I ran into a huge lorry which landed in a ditch. I was fine, but very shaken. An army Land Rover, which was right behind me, stopped and its occupants came to my aid. They took me to the local police station, fed me with coffee and gave me a lift to Nairobi. Among my rescuers was the major of the 32nd Field Squadron Royal Engineers who, on hearing where I worked, said that he had five men who hadn't anything to do in the immediate future. Was there any building work, maintenance or painting they could do? Of course there was, they could, and they did! I saw at first hand the care and compassion our armed forces had for the people of Kenya.

God even worked through Kenyan Customs officials! My car, without which I might never have met Lorna and Betty, arrived in Mombasa in a transit bond to Uganda. Missionaries coming to work in Kenya could get all their belongings into the country duty-free in the first three months after their arrival. This meant I had three months to get the car released from the transit bond and imported into Kenya. On paper that sounds simple; in reality it was a nightmare. Every week I was in Nairobi at Customs and Excise, and every week the papers were either lost or held up in one of the many departments through which they had to pass. The three months were history before the great day came when I had clearance to import the car on payment of what seemed to me a vast amount of duty. At that stage all I wanted was for the whole procedure to be finished. It would be cheap at the price! By the time I had all the papers stamped in all the relevant places by each of the required departments it was 3 p.m.. With great anticipation I went confidently to pay my money when the grill was suddenly pulled down and I was told abruptly, 'We can't take money after 3 p.m.. Come back tomorrow!'

I was so tired and frustrated and angry that I started to cry. Having started, I couldn't stop! As I sobbed and sobbed someone rushed to get me a chair. Then a wad of toilet paper was thrust into my hand to blow my nose.

'I am so sorry,' I apologised. 'It's just that I work far away helping wee disabled Maasai children. It's difficult to leave the children to come into Nairobi and this is taking up so much of my time.'

Then I remembered the photos I had just collected of the first children who had learned to walk. I passed them round the officials.

'This is Sirinoi,' sniff, sniff, 'and he has just learned to walk. And this is Lesianka. He can't walk yet but he can stand by himself with the help of his calipers and crutches.'

Seeing the men's faces soften, and realising their change of heart, I asked, 'Is there absolutely no way I could pay today, so I don't have to leave the children again tomorrow?'

'Just a moment,' an official said. 'The papers have gone for authorisation.'

A short time later, while I was drinking a cup of steaming 'chai,' a beaming official came into the office and said, 'You can go now, the payment has been waived. Thank you for helping our children in Kenya. May God bless you in your work!'

I started to cry all over again! God is so good.

Answered prayer

On another occasion God helped in getting a very special wheelchair into Kenya. We had recently admitted a wee boy who, when falling out of a tree, broke his back and was paralysed from the waist down. He came to us with horrendous bedsores. Over the months while they were healing his position needed to be changed frequently. Some people in the U.K. whose child had died had donated a big heavy chair that could be put into any position from upright to flat like a bed. A special cushion to prevent bedsores was also given which, of course, added to the weight of it. I had to go on a short visit to the U.K. and decided just to bring it back to Kenya with me. Unfortunately British Airways refused to take it free. Each time I called they said it would cost £600 to airfreight the chair to Kenya. I decided to have one last attempt and arranged for the wheelchair to be brought to me at Heathrow. Many people were praying. As I checked in my suitcase I said, 'I also have this wheelchair. It will be on your computer because I have telephoned British Airways several times but they've refused to take it free. It's for a poor wee Maasai boy who fell out of a tree and is paralysed. Is there any way you could take it free of charge?'

'Okay,' said the check-in person without hesitation, and he called for someone to label the chair and take it away. I was left just standing with my mouth open! What a great encouragement for all the people who were praying, many at that very moment.

On arrival at Jomo Kenyatta Airport I took possession of the chair and walked through the 'something to declare' line.

'What do you have to declare?' the customs official asked fiercely.

'This wheelchair, 40 dolls, 80 toy cars and 20 watches,' I said as confidently as I could. He frowned at me and, just as I was wondering how I would talk myself through this situation, the big sliding doors of the arrival hall opened and there was a line of children with their calipers and crutches, all waving excitedly to me. Now it was easy.

'The dolls and cars are Christmas presents for these poor wee disabled children,' I explained. 'And the watches are for the staff who look after them.'

His frown lifted. 'Okay, have a very happy Christmas.'

I became quite expert at using the plea, 'but I work with poor wee disabled children,' to produce kindness and prompt help. It got me out of many scrapes over the years!

Rev. Alec Aitken

Georgie was with us in Edinburgh each furlough and I was involved in her returns to Africa on several occasions. We would go to the airport knowing full well that her luggage was well over the weight allowance, as she took back medicines, crutches, supplies, and even wheelchairs. Having helped her unload the cases etc. at the check-in desk, our task was to pray that she would be allowed to take the excess through. And every time, to the best of my knowledge, Georgie was able to take all her luggage without penalty right through to Kenya. God did hear and answer prayer concerning this, not just once, but on several occasions. We saw miracles taking place before our very eyes! Often I may have doubted, but I don't think Georgie really did. She went forward in faith.

She had a deep and unshakeable faith that God would undertake, not only in matters of excess baggage, but also in all matters of financial support. It was almost a taboo subject which she refused to discuss. And to talk about it at all was a matter of real embarrassment to her. Georgie had then, and still has, a clear faith and assurance that God will provide, an assurance which she has seen vindicated again and again.

God supplied my needs, and the needs of the Child Care Centre, in many different ways. He was so gracious and especially gentle in the early years when I often didn't even know what I needed. The right thing or right person just arrived at the right time. One day a Maasai lady arrived at the Centre carrying a little boy with plasters on both feet. She handed me a letter from a doctor in Nairobi which read, 'Please remove these plasters and fit this child with orthopaedic boots.' As I had just bought my first pair of plaster shears I removed the plasters confidently. The child's feet were tiny! He had undergone surgery for bilateral clubfeet, and I knew that without proper support his feet would quickly return to their old position, but I seriously doubted that I could find as small a size as he needed. Without much hope I tried on a pair of size three boots, the smallest size of polio boots available in Kenya. They were far too big. I returned to the store wondering, 'Where on earth will I get a pair of boots smaller than a size three?'

I was actually thinking those words when I saw a box that had been brought by our R.A.F. friends the previous day. I wondered what it held and, as I opened it, my hopes rose! To my joy, right on top was a tiny pair of white orthopaedic boots with a label tied on them saying, 'Smaller than size three!' I rushed to where I had left the wee boy and put the boots on him. Had they been made to measure they couldn't have fitted any more perfectly! There were even little straps on the inside, in exactly the right places to hold the child's feet in the correct position. I was overwhelmed by the wonder of our Lord's loving care of our needy children. These boots had been donated months before in the U.K., taken to Lyneham Air Base, held there for a flight to bring them to Kenya and then transported from Nairobi to Kajiado, all orchestrated just so that a wee Maasai boy could have the boots he needed at exactly the time he needed them. Amazing! Over and over again God has been wonderfully proved to be true to his word, 'Before they call I will answer; while they are still speaking I will hear' (Isa. 65:24).

ROYAL AIR FORCE NEWS
June 28 – July 11 1985.
KAJIADO – Helping the children
When you next pass through the arrivals lounge at Lyneham spare a few moments to take a closer look

at the large picture board covered in photographs of happy smiling African children. They live at the Kajiado Child Care Centre outside Nairobi and they are a far cry from the children presently facing starvation and death in Ethiopia.

Kajiado is a success story, but to keep those faces smiling the Centre needs money, so dig deep into your pockets for all those foreign coins the banks refuse to change and put them into the charity jar close by – the United Kingdom Mobile Air Movements Squadron (U.K.M.A.M.S.) based at Lyneham will be grateful and so will the children.

Throughout 'Operation Bushel,' the famine mercy mission, teams from the base and mobile flights of U.K.M.A.M.S. have been in Ethiopia helping to move millions of pounds of relief supplies in the desperate attempt to save lives. But for many of the men serving with U.K.M.A.M.S., Ethiopia is not their first African experience – the Squadron has now been supporting Kajiado as its main charity for around five years.

The Centre is run by Georgie Orme and caters for around 100 disabled children, mainly the victims of polio and rickets. They come from the vast Maasai homelands of Kenya where their families are so poor they cannot care for them properly. They are forced to travel hundreds of miles to reach Kajiado where they receive all the treatment and operations they need. They return to their families just three times a year.

U.K.M.A.M.S. is not the only group to lend its support to Kajiado, but it must be one of the most enthusiastic. The Squadron began helping in just a small way, but more recently has bought equipment for the small workshop at the Centre and is presently trying to raise enough money for a small cement mixer and spare parts for Kajiado's Land Rover. Most of the money comes from the charity jar in the arrivals lounge, but the Squadron's enthusiasm for the Child Care Centre has rubbed off on others and now groups, including an ATC squadron and a Brownie pack in the Lyneham area are busily doing their bit to help the children.

'Whenever it's possible we like to get some of our members out there to see the work the Centre does,' explained Wing Commander Bob Dixon, OC U.K.M.A.M.S., 'and the place never fails to have a deep effect on them. They come back full of it, realising what a special place it is. The children are handicapped, but it remains a very happy place where they get the treatment and tender loving care they need.'

5
And God gave us Daniel

The first impression that a visitor to the Child Care Centre had was of CRUTCHES – it seemed that everyone used them! Wee girls swung along speedily, others struggled, boys hopped around playing football, using one crutch as an extra leg with a longer reach! That perception of the place was because the majority of admissions were children with paralysis following infection with the polio virus. Usually the children, having developed a febrile illness, were taken to the local dispensary. As most common fevers were due to malaria, the nurse would give intramuscular chloroquine into the buttocks to treat the suspected malaria. Parents nearly always came with that story, convinced that the paralysis of the leg, not noticed before the visit to the dispensary, had been caused by the injection.

Nchaa was such a child. Both arms and legs were paralysed and she had bad scoliosis of the spine. Following polio the muscles which bend the leg are often less affected by the paralysis than those which straighten it, therefore the limb is held in flexion. Then the tendons at the ankle, knee and hip shorten and become contracted. Nchaa

Georgie with Nchaa whose arms and legs were badly affected by polio.

had contractures of both hips and knees and the Achilles tendons. These had to be stretched every day, to the point of pain and just beyond. I was as gentle as I could be but, to wee Nchaa, it was very painful. Over many weeks her legs were gradually straightened enough to be strapped into calipers. Even then her hips were unstable and her spine badly curved. Just at that time I received a gift from a Brownie pack in the south of England. When gifts came from children I always tried to use them for something special and then let them know how their gift had helped. So I took Nchaa to the very expensive invalid equipment shop in Nairobi where there was a skilled technician. He made a plaster cast of her body and moulded a leather corset to fit her back exactly. This corset was then attached to specially made calipers that held her legs straight and her body upright. After a great deal of practise Nchaa was able to balance and then eventually walk with crutches.

'Now that you can walk, Nchaa, you won't be carried to nursery school any more,' I told her. All the children who were too young for school, or couldn't walk to the primary schools, went to our nursery school along with other children from the local community. The path from dormitory to nursery school was twenty five yards long; from Nchaa's point of view it might as well have been twenty five miles. But one special day saw her walking, persevering inch by inch, with me walking backwards in front of her egging her on, while Ng'oto Samuel came behind, both of us ready to catch her if she fell or to hold her when she needed a rest. When at last, after a full forty minutes, she arrived at the nursery school door all the other children clapped and cheered. Every morning thereafter she struggled along the path, taking a little less time each day.

It wasn't very long before Nchaa raised her sights even higher.

'I want to go to big school now,' she said. 'I'm too old for nursery school.'

'You can't go to the primary school until you're able to get yourself up if you fall.' I told her. 'The teachers are too busy to lift you all the time.'

For many weeks I watched her from my window. The brave wee girl would walk a short distance, drop her crutches and then fall to the ground. I watched as she struggled to get one crutch and use it to balance and push herself up before reaching out for the second one and then stand upright. She repeated that over and over again. She didn't know I was watching her, or how much I admired her pluck. As it became clear that she was going to achieve her goal eventually, we started thinking about the practicalities of her attending primary school. The major problem was the toilet. The school toilet was a long drop – a hole in the ground, and she was unable to squat. So we had a special raised toilet with a seat built for her and others like her. Nchaa went on to complete primary schooling and vocational training in tailoring. She became one of the first people in Kenya to have her spine straightened and strengthened by the insertion of Harrington rods, a technique brought to Kijabe Hospital years later.

The daily routine of the Child Care Centre continued, with me doing inspection each morning to make sure the dormitories were tidied before the children went to school. Training in self-reliance was high on our agenda. As soon as children were able to put on their own calipers and boots they were encouraged to do so. They cleaned their boots and shoes and made their own beds, if they were physically able, and even helped with washing dishes. As the number of children wearing calipers and crutches increased, so did the number of trips into Nairobi for repairs. It became essential to find a local shoemaker for the simpler repairs. One day in town we found a shoemaker who was a Maasai and was disabled himself. He was ideal for us, especially as he would understand the problems of the disabled.

A bad start

When Daniel was two years old he contracted polio and his legs were badly affected. His disability meant that he couldn't do the work of a Maasai boy. He couldn't herd his father's precious cattle – a tragedy for a boy from his background. And that was the second tragedy in his short life. Daniel's mother was his father's first wife, and he was her first child. That should have set him up in a prestigious position as firstborn of his father, but it didn't, because he wasn't born until his father's second wife had borne two children. Ousted from his position in the family because of his mother's barrenness in the first few years of her marriage, and then ousted from his position as a herder, Daniel spent his time with his mother and the other women and felt that his father despised him.

One day a government official went to Daniel's area to persuade the elders to allow one child from every family to go to school. The Maasai resisted education because their children were needed for the much more important job of caring for their animals. However, the government had charged the Maasai chiefs to promote education and they had to do their best to do so. Daniel's father was approached about sending one of his children to school. Of course, the one he chose was Daniel. There was no point in sending a child who would be useful at home. Whatever Daniel's father was thinking, God had his hand on the boy and he became a Christian during his primary school education. Daniel had sustained paralysis of both legs and walked with two sticks. Although he did well at primary school, his father wouldn't pay fees for him to continue with secondary education. Instead, he did a shoemaking course at a government sponsored training centre. It was while he was there he met Lydia, who would later become his wife. She, also disabled, trained to be a seamstress.

As there was always work to be done on the children's shoes Daniel was later invited to work part-time at the Child Care Centre and part-time for himself. When he agreed to do that I bought a leather-work sewing machine for his use. By then he and Lydia were married and Lorna arranged for the building of two little rooms for them. One room was their living quarters and the other Daniel's workshop. This arrangement not only suited me, as I didn't have to go into town to have the children's shoes repaired, but it was a real blessing for the young couple.

Before very long Daniel's contribution became so valuable that he stopped working for himself and became a full-time member of staff. He moved on from just repairing the children's shoes to maintaining their calipers and crutches. So adept did he become at caring for their calipers that eventually he was all but remaking them. The only thing that prevented him actually constructing calipers was his inability to bend the metal rods in the required way. It seemed only sensible to train him to do this and to make the calipers our children needed in-house. So Daniel was sent for a week to the A.P.D.K. workshop in Nairobi and was taught how to bend the steel rods.

Lorna designed a lean-to workshop outside the main workshop where he could bend the metal. I scoured the Nairobi industrial area (my least favourite job) for bright steel rods of varying sizes, leather, buckles, tools, and all the other necessary materials, and then persuaded a Nairobi firm that made mattresses to donate their off-cuts of foam for padding the tops of the calipers. Boots were bought direct from the Bata shoe company and we found an engineering firm to make the metal attachment that went into the boot to hold the caliper in place. Two special metal rod-benders were made, and with those and a vice, plus another short course in welding, coupled with the gift of an arc welder by U.K.M.A.M.S., Daniel was able to make his first caliper. What a great day that was!

Daniel Ole Sapayia with a child wearing the first calipers made at Kajiado

A surprise gift

While I was searching for people who could show me how best to care for disabled children I heard that A.P.D.K. had a school for children with disabilities down at the coast. When I visited I asked about their physiotherapy programme and was told, 'Oh! We don't do exercises. We just encourage the children to swim in the sea every day.' 'That's fine,' I thought, 'if you live beside the sea. Sometimes we can hardly find enough water for everyone to drink! Even the rivers are dry.' About a year later we had a visit from the chairman of Round Table 21 in Nairobi. He explained that the previous year had been International Year of the Disabled, and they had a considerable amount of money left in their account which couldn't be carried over to this year's project. It could only be used on a project for the disabled. The wife of a Round Table member, who had visited the Child Care Centre, told him that we needed a hydrotherapy pool! Maybe we did … but we hadn't even thought of praying for one!

I have to confess to being sceptical about the whole business. 'Where would we get the water?' was only one of the questions that kept surfacing in my mind. I was slightly reassured when I learnt that with the addition of chemicals the water only needed topping up rather than changing. Round Table also promised us that they would put in solar water-heating panels so that the water would be comfortably warm for therapy. The project went ahead, and with great ceremony the first hydrotherapy pool in Kenya was opened by two members of parliament. By then I had been back to the U.K. on home assignment and had found a very friendly physiotherapy department that gave me a short course on simple hydrotherapy. The pool was absolutely wonderful for the children as they had such freedom in the water without their constricting calipers and boots. It made their therapy fun. Helped by the buoyancy of the water they were often able to get movement that they could never have achieved on dry land and then do further work on it. We saw tremendous improvement in mobility, confidence and freedom in many otherwise restricted children.

As time went on we found ourselves dealing with children with more and more complicated problems. Also our older children were growing so much taller that travelling on public transport sitting with their legs strapped up straight became a problem. Daniel was beginning to puzzle how he could make a caliper that bent at the knee. Just then, in God's perfect timing, we had a visit from some people from the Tanzanian Training Centre for Orthopaedics Technologists (T.A.T.C.O.T.), a department in the Kilimanjaro Christian Medical Centre in Tanzania. They were looking for patients for their third year students who were about to sit final examinations and they had heard about our work and wondered if we might have five or six children with suitable problems.

Daniel and I were so thrilled at the prospect of this help that we didn't stop to think about how many problems we would face. The East African Union of Kenya, Tanzania and Uganda was no longer functioning in anything but name and we needed travel documents for everyone. It was no problem for me; I had my passport. But neither Daniel nor any of the five children had birth certificates, let alone passports. Thankfully, we had a Maasai friend who was an immigration officer and he was able to help us get the necessary documentation.

The drive was magnificent, south to Arusha and into the arms of another Maasai family, Tanzanian this time, who cooked and cared for us. As always God had his people in the right places at the right time to help us on our way! We passed Mount Meru, and then drove east to Moshi on the southern foothills of the snow-capped Mount Kilimanjaro. The students in T.A.T.C.O.T. were excited to see us and get their first look at their final exam patients. The children stayed in Moshi Chapel, a children's home run by a Scotsman from the Christian Brethren. They were picked up each morning, taken to the hospital and generally made a great fuss of. At the end of three weeks they were all returned with beautiful professionally made appliances. One boy, Tumate, had been born with a perfectly formed lower leg, but attached to his hip! His was the most complicated orthosis, with his own foot in a plastic splint at knee level, and another artificial one where his foot should have been. Tumate was thrilled as he was able to run about and play football just like the other boys.

Seper wearing Daniel's first knee-bending caliper

The great thing, or so we thought at the time, was that T.A.T.C.O.T. agreed to take Daniel for a three-month course on making knee-bending calipers. This could have solved the problem our taller children were experiencing in class and, more especially, on public transport. Even in my car a boy would sometimes be sitting on the back seat with his foot resting on the top of the seat in front as there was no room for it in the back! T.A.T.C.O.T.'s method of making these calipers was, unfortunately, very expensive. It involved making a plaster mould of the leg and then fitting the caliper on to that. All the materials were imported from Germany, as was the equipment for making the calipers. It was all away beyond our budget. Daniel was disappointed and thought that his three months training had been wasted. But in God's economy nothing is ever wasted, as Daniel was to discover some time later.

A.I.C. CHILD CARE CENTRE,
P.O. BOX 25, KAJIADO, KENYA

1984

… From a very select wee group of twenty children in the Child Care Centre.

Twelve children had surgery in February by a visiting orthopaedic surgeon and all are in plaster.

The children enjoy the extra attention they have in the holidays. Next week we'll take a picnic lunch and watch the East African Safari Rally, and another day we'll visit the game park.

I wish you could be here to listen to the squeals of joy as the children play and exercise in the hydrotherapy pool. They just love the water and the freedom it gives them to move without the burden of calipers. I can already see an improvement in the little ones especially, as muscles hitherto unused get some movement, helped by the buoyancy of the water.

I have spent a frustrating few weeks trying to get Kimendere, our oldest boy, established in a secondary school, by no means the straightforward process it is in the U.K.. As a temporary measure, he is attending a private school in town. This means he has a walk of one mile each day – not easy with calipers and crutches. Pray that he will soon get a place boarding in a school near us.

The building of our much-needed dormitory has started and I praise the Lord for funds to complete it. The staff and all seventy-eight children have remained well this term, apart from problems with the lice that came back from the holidays – even I caught them!

The Nursery School feeding programme at Eiti is in full swing – the children look so sweet drinking their Scots Porridge Oats from brightly coloured plastic mugs. School is held under a tree and writing practise is done in the dust. The parents are trying hard to raise enough money for a little school building.

Daniel and I had a very helpful visit to the Tanzania Training Centre for Orthopaedic Technologists in Moshi. They have offered to take Daniel for three months training next year and at the moment four of our children are there, being fitted for below-knee prostheses.

I was dreading the thought of spending the money the Lord had sent on the wrong tools for the workshop. Gordon McCullough arrived from Northern Ireland en route to Uganda and helped me buy the right ones! He 'just happened' to be in Kenya a few weeks later when I was setting up the workshop and he came to advise on the best place for drills, benches and metal cutter.

Continue to pray for Nancy (my colleague who came after Lorna and Betty left); she is doing very well with Maasai and at present is with Lorna and Betty for five weeks as part of her language learning programme.

With love,
Georgie

6
Special Children

Word had spread like wildfire that children were being helped at Kajiado. We could have been inundated with every needy child in the district. The chiefs in the different areas knew the people in their care and encouraged parents to bring any children with physical disabilities to the Child Care Centre. But we couldn't help every child or even every kind of disability. We had to restrict ourselves to physical disabilities as we had neither the staff nor the expertise to care for those with brain damage or learning difficulties, and we aimed to be a short-term rehabilitation centre for those whose disabilities could be helped.

Shomet was a blessing to us while he was in the Child Care Centre, but time proved that he was better at home with his family. This is his story. One day a Maasai man came with something hidden under the large red blanket that he wore. When he tried to open the blanket to show us what was there, from the piercing cries and the panic-stricken struggle we guessed the child he was hiding was very disturbed.

Tigirayu! the father ordered sternly, *Tupuku!* ('Be quiet and come out'). The wee boy stopped yelling and came out! In fact, he turned out to be very bright, bright enough on that day to know that an unknown white lady could be dangerous. As we saw more of him we realised he was older than he seemed, but he suffered from dwarfism and osteogenesis imperfecta, or brittle bone disease. Shomet was a dear wee boy, who

Shomet has dwarfism and osteogenesis imperfecta – and a guitar!

did well at school despite frequent absences, and was very receptive spiritually. Although he longed to join in with the other boys playing football, his bones broke so easily it was too big a risk to take. A simple trip would break a bone. Several times the boy fractured his femur, was admitted to hospital, put in traction and then discharged back to us in a hip spica plaster cast, only to fall and break another bone! One Sunday afternoon I felt so sorry for him confined to bed encased in plaster that I put him in a reclining wheelchair, all securely padded with pillows, in order that he could be outside with the other children.

I had just settled down to my usual cup of afternoon

tea when a huge retinue of boys appeared at my door.

'Shomet has fallen out of the wheelchair,' they said excitedly. I couldn't believe it. Shomet couldn't even move! How could he have fallen out? It transpired that as soon as my back was turned the boys started playing racing cars with his wheelchair to brighten his life up a bit. When a wheel hit a stone at full speed the wheelchair overturned and Shomet was lying beside it screaming in agony. After getting him some strong pain relief, we set out on the long two-and-a-half-hour drive to Kijabe Hospital. The last four kilometres was a steep bumpy downhill track and he screamed at every bump. We were both wrecks, for different reasons, by the time we reached the hospital. It was midnight, the doctor looked at Shomet totally encased in plaster of Paris up to his armpits … and with one arm broken. Then he looked at me. I'm sure he thought I was totally unfit to be caring for children! When Shomet healed it was agreed that it would be kinder for him to stay at home away from our very 'rough' disabled boys in Kajiado. We missed his plucky, bright personality, but as news filtered through about him from time to time, we were encouraged to hear that he was known by all as a determined, witnessing Christian.

Some children were brought to us whom we couldn't help but were able to find hospitals in Nairobi for them. Burns were sadly very common as all cooking in a Maasai house is done on the floor. Three stones are laid out to form a support for the cooking pot and a long log stays in the fire all the time so that the fire can be rekindled quickly by blowing on it. It's very easy for a child either to trip over the log or crawl or fall into the fire.

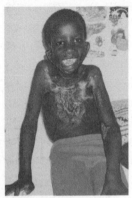

Leshinka, his chin fused to his chest following a burning accident

One wee boy, Leshinka, had been wearing a nylon sweater over his *shuka* when he went past the fire and his cloth caught alight. As the other children tried to pull the cloth over his head the melting nylon stuck under his chin and he was terribly burned. When Leshinka arrived at the Centre after many months in hospital there was so much scarring that the scar tissue had shortened and had pulled his chin right down on to his chest wall. It took many months of plastic surgery to release all the scar tissue, and many more months of patient therapy to make sure that the scars didn't reform. But by the time he left us Leshinka was able to hold his head up once again.

Leshinka, head held high, on the swing

'I finded a louse!'

One day a request came from Kajiado District Hospital for us to take a wee girl who was in a hip spica cast and cried all the time. Naishorua had been admitted to Kenyatta National hospital in Nairobi with burns to her arms and upper body. When at last she was allowed out of bed she fell, dislocated her hip, and was put into the cast. Kenyatta National Hospital, needing the beds, transferred Naishorua to Kajiado for the three months she would be in plaster. When Naishorua came to the Child Care Centre it quickly became apparent why she cried all the time – the plaster was full of lice! I discovered this at a weekend, and only had chicken lice powder for the chickens Lorna reared for their eggs, but I shook the powder in round the top of the plaster cast and up from the bottom. When I eventually got her to the orthopaedic clinic in Nairobi the doctor asked, 'Where has this child been? She should have been back six months ago to have her cast off!' The plaster had been on for nine months! No wonder it was full of lice.

When the doctor proceeded to cut the cast off with an electric rotating plaster cutter Naishorua was terrified. As soon as the cast was off I lifted her up into my arms to cuddle and comfort her. To my horror I saw a heap of squirming lice which had congregated round her knee to escape the lice powder. I got Naishorua cleaned up and thought no more of it. Days later Mary, a very dear large Kikuyu lady who helped me in the house, was ironing my dress. She showed it to me triumphantly, and said, 'I finded a louse!' It was the first, but not the last time I became infested. In fact, it was something of an occupational hazard!

Other challenges

At the beginning and end of each school term our compound seemed to erupt, with children running everywhere. Our six hearing-impaired children congregated at the Centre at the beginning of each term for me to drive them to the Kambui School for the Deaf just north of Nairobi. They were just normal, rough but bigger children who took very little heed of our disabled wee ones. Shouting at them did no good at all because they couldn't hear! And it was hard to catch their attention as they moved so quickly in their excitement at being back with their friends who could communicate in sign language. The drive to the school for the deaf was very beautiful, green and lush, as the road wound through rich coffee plantations. But trying to keep my eyes on the treacherous, muddy road, with six children poking me and signing to point out exciting things on the way was well-nigh impossible!

Most of these children had lost their hearing following meningitis and still retained some speech. I took all children who came to us with ear problems to the E.N.T. Department at Kenyatta National Hospital where there was a very helpful doctor. He examined their ears, fishing out unmentionable objects like flies, ticks, beads and even beans before they could be assessed by audiogram to see if fitting them with hearing aids would allow them to attend normal school, or if they needed to be in a special school for the deaf. Unfortunately Kambui School insisted on oral communication and didn't encourage signing. This was a real problem for our children who had grown up only hearing the Maasai language. As all classes in school were in English to comply with government policy, our children had to learn to lip-read a foreign language, never having heard it before. Also, because the school was in a Kikuyu area, all the chatter around them was in Kikuyu or Swahili. So the children mostly lost whatever Maasai speech they had and thus found it difficult to communicate when they came home for holidays. We did a great deal of campaigning to get a unit for those who were hearing impaired in Kajiado but, although much was promised, no unit ever materialised. After a few years it seemed kinder not to take on any more new deaf children but rather let them stay at home. We felt it was better for them to be herds-boys or girls helping at home rather than lose their speech in their home-tongue and whatever Maasai language lip-reading skills they had acquired.

There was an excellent unit for the visually handicapped at the local boys' primary school where children were taught by a blind teacher. I always wondered how Mr Mwango could teach Maanda, our first completely blind boy. They had no common language, and lessons were in English. But Maanda learnt quickly, and soon he was reading with his fingers, writing on his Braille typewriter and integrated into a sighted class. Mr Mwango was a good disciplinarian, and when he became headmaster of the whole primary school he really licked our physically disabled naughty boys into shape. He made absolutely no concessions for disability. He had made it himself the hard way; so could they!

Medical problems

Another huge problem we often came across was tuberculosis of the bone. A child would come with a history of a wound which had drained pus for many months and wouldn't heal. Usually on x-ray the hip joint was found to be destroyed by the infection. The child then needed eighteen months of medication and weeks of painful dressings, packing the sinuses to be sure that they healed from the inside out. When at last the infection was healed, surgery was required to fuse the hip joint. That was followed by three months in a hip spica cast. We didn't keep those children when their treatment was completed as they didn't need follow-up care. When they were healed and mobile we all rejoiced and they were discharged.

The most visually dramatic results from surgery were seen on children with cleft lip and palate. One nine-year-old was brought to us horribly disfigured with a cleft lip and palate and teeth all twisted and protruding. He had been

Lemayian before surgery for a cleft lip

Lemayian after surgery

named Loleleo, which means a piece of broken gourd. Our Flying Doctor friends found a free bed and a kind surgeon for him in Gertrude's

Gardens, an excellent private children's hospital in Nairobi. After three operations to reconstruct his mouth, he turned into a really handsome wee boy. When his father first saw him he glowed with joy and promptly changed his name to Lemayian, the blessed one!

Skin problems were very hard to cope with in a Maasai village. As water is always at a premium, not much is wasted on washing. Anyway there is so much dust and so many flies spreading infection that treating skin infections was a losing battle. Maripet was brought with sores all over his body and he didn't respond to any of the usual treatments. In desperation I took him to Dr Colin Forbes, a private paediatrician in Nairobi. Dr Forbes was a dear man who was interested in all that we were doing. I only took the more complicated cases to him and he received them with kindness and never charged for tests or treatments.

Dr Forbes diagnosed Maripet's condition as being an autoimmune disease. The boy's immune system, instead of attacking infection, was attacking and destroying his body, causing his huge sores. He was admitted to Gertrude's Gardens and treated with steroids to dampen down his immune system. After discharge Maripet was all healed up, but his temperature had to be checked every morning and evening. Any rise could indicate infection and necessitated a reduction of his steroids, which then caused his skin to erupt. It was a constant struggle to get the benefit of the medication and yet keep him free of infection. There were many times when I was on the phone to Dr Forbes daily. Even when he was admitted to hospital, Dr Forbes found donors to pay the bills.

Sorrows and joys

Maripet's mother cared for him beautifully. At the end of each school holiday she brought him back from their traditional Maasai house immaculate, having carried out all the treatments to the letter. For several years we passed him back from one of us to the other and developed a real bond. Maripet must have felt really ill much of the time, but he never complained and always insisted on going to school. Eventually, when I was on holiday with my minister and his wife from Scotland, I received a phone call to say that Maripet had been admitted to Gertrude Gardens. He went downhill very quickly and died. I felt awful; neither his mother nor I had been with him. By the time I returned to Kajiado Maripet's older brothers had arranged his burial. The grave had been dug behind Kajiado Hospital. I couldn't understand it; why was he not to be buried at home? The brothers, fearing his body being buried at home, had told their mother that I wanted him buried at Kajiado! She thought I meant at the Child Care Centre and agreed. Eventually, realising she had been tricked, Maripet's mother managed to get a lift to Kajiado and arrived just as I did. The poor woman clung to me. 'Please don't let him be buried in the bush. Please bury him in the Child Care Centre!' she pled. The brothers were adamant, and we were mere women who had no say. Maripet's grave had been dug and, according to their tradition, if they didn't use it someone else would die. The full horror of death to those who have no faith in Christ hit me. Dear Maripet loved the Lord. I knew he was safely in heaven, but his poor mother had no such comfort.

Kumoin was a granny's child. In fact, it was his granny's cries for help to Lorna and Betty that sparked off the starting of the Child Care Centre. He had paralysis of his right arm and leg, possibly following cerebral malaria. As he became older his good leg grew at a normal rate but his paralysed leg didn't, which meant he needed an ever-increasing raise to his shoe to keep his legs an equal length. A visiting orthopaedic surgeon was keen to operate on Kumoin in order to slow down the growth in his good leg. The boy was suspicious of surgery to his good leg, but eventually agreed. Sadly, the growth slowed down on the outside of the leg but not on the inside, resulting in a very marked knock-knee. The poor boy needed a crutch to help him walk, and the crutch occupied his better arm. Eventually he had further surgery to straighten his leg and, while he was in hospital, word came that his mother had died.

'Why is all this happening to me?' he cried, as I drove him back to his home village to be with his family. The rain was pouring down as we crossed what had been a dry river bed. The water came rushing down and the level rose rapidly. We were at the mercy of a flash flood when, to my horror, the engine cut out! Kumoin had one leg in a caliper and the other in a full cast. There was no way he could get out of the car. People standing on the bank watched helplessly. I just cried to the Lord, 'Help us!' and turned the key one more time. The engine started and we got out of the river safely.

Kumoin's mother had died two weeks previously, after giving birth to a baby boy two weeks before that. A relative had taken in all her other children but didn't know how to cope with the baby. The infant, who was being fed cow's milk from a gourd with a teat on the end, had developed diarrhoea and vomiting and weighed only two kilos at one month old. Not wanting any more disasters to befall Kumoin, it was agreed that I would take his baby brother back to Kajiado with us. We got into the car, which was so waterlogged it wouldn't start. So that night the three of us slept in the village, all cuddled up together on a cowskin – if one can cuddle up with a boy with plaster on one leg and a caliper on the other, along with a baby with diarrhoea and vomiting! Next morning, when the car still wouldn't start, we hitched a lift on the back of a passing pickup: Kumoin, Kuntayo and myself, along with the goat I had been given as a thank you for taking the sick baby with me. Eventually, after being stuck many times in the mud, we made it safely back to Kajiado. The mechanic sent out to rescue the car spent three days drying it out before it would start. God had graciously and miraculously rescued us from that flash flood.

Never could we have guessed how much joy Kuntayo would bring to our lives

Nancy (right) and Georgie with Kuntayo.

as Nancy and I took him into our home because the Child Care Centre wasn't set up to care for a tiny baby without his mother. He wormed his way right into our hearts. One of the hardest things I had to do was to give Kuntayo all the love he needed and yet be prepared to part with him later because he had a family. Although we hope that one day he will go back to be part of his family Anna, who was housekeeper in the Centre, 'adopted' Kuntayo when he was little into her family and brought him up as one of her own.

Meanwhile Kumoin started secondary school but found the other boys unkind and unhelpful. When standing in line for his meals he couldn't carry his plate to the table with one arm paralysed and the other holding his crutch. Life wasn't easy for Kumoin then, and it hasn't grown any easier to this day.

Rev. Alec Aitken on his sabbatical spent in Kenya
I had the great privilege of visiting Georgie and seeing the work at first hand for a period of six weeks. What stands out for me of this time? Georgie was always immensely busy with care and oversight of the children in the Centre, and she appeared to me to be a real mother figure to them. The respect and high esteem of the staff and children was very obvious. My friend knew all the children intimately, their different needs and personalities, and she was as firm as a good parent should be. When making home visits to the Maasai villages she was always received with love and gratitude for all that she was doing for the children. This was obvious one day as we returned from a village complete with a live goat as a present for Naado.

The goat subsequently appeared at her house in an aluminium basin all neatly butchered and with its head adorning the pile of meat.

There were times when I was able to observe closely Georgie's emotional involvement in the lives of the children. We visited one young boy in hospital in Nairobi who was gravely ill. His condition was a matter of much pain to her as he deteriorated and subsequently died. In the events of the funeral arrangements I have never seen my friend so distressed and upset. The boy's mother's wishes were swept aside by other family members as her son was buried in the local township cemetery. What happened that day pained and grieved Georgie more deeply than I can express. The suffering and sorrow of the mother was also her suffering and her sorrow as she sought to comfort her during that time. Such was the cost of Georgie's ministry in the care of the children.

7
You can't squash a louse with one finger

Lorna and Betty, who welcomed me into their hearts and into their ministry at Kajiado, were extraordinary colleagues. Although they were very different they worked really well together, and they had great hearts for those who had been missed out from the advance of the gospel. One day Betty came into my house. 'I have something to tell you,' she said solemnly. 'Lorna and I believe that the Lord is leading us to work with the Njemps people who live near Lake Baringo. There are many on the far side of the lake who have never had the opportunity to hear about Jesus.' I was absolutely devastated. How could I ever cope without them? We had only had three years working together. In that time, not only had they made it their business to build up my shattered self-confidence, but they had also done a huge amount of work in the Child Care Centre. Betty and I sat on the floor and cried together. I just couldn't imagine being without them. Apart from anything else Lorna and Betty had dealt with the swarms of visitors who descended on us to admire our lovely wee disabled children playing football and singing. How would I cope with baking cakes and biscuits and serving tea at the same time as answering all their questions?

The only thing I wouldn't miss was Lorna's chickens. She thought it was a good idea to buy day-old chicks and rear them to give eggs to supplement the children's protein intake. We had several batches of a hundred. It was really the only thing we didn't see eye to eye about. For one thing Lorna and Betty were often away somewhere when the electricity went off and I would be left trying to keep the hundred chicks alive and warm with paraffin lamps and hot water bottles. Then when the chickens were a bit older my cat Ndorrop, 'the short one', was found with feathers on his whiskers and accused of eating them. He had been, but of course I had to be loyal to my beloved cat! At least now I would be able just to buy eggs with no argument.

When Lorna and Betty left, Ng'oto Samuel insisted I needed a partner, quoting a Maasai proverb: 'You can't squash a louse with one finger.' While nobody could take my friends' place, the Lord had been speaking to a friend of theirs in South Africa who used to arrange meetings for A.I.M. missionaries on home assignment when they were in Durban. Nancy McElroy, a teacher of the deaf, felt God calling her to work in Kajiado, but at that time it was difficult for South Africans to get visas and work permits to come into Kenya. We prayed, believing that if God wanted Nancy to come to Kajiado he would remove all the barriers. Nancy was sure she would get the papers because she was certain the Lord was calling her. It took eight months, and in Ng'oto Samuel's words, 'We had to believe and believe and believe'. Nancy received her papers at the very last moment, quite literally, as she was about to go through the boarding door to fly to Kenya. As a result she was given the Maasai name *Nairuko*, 'the one who believed!'

Nancy's first assignment was to give six months to Maasai language study. As well as studying, memorising and imitating, she was to learn phrases and go round the town and villages talking Maasai (just those sentences, relevant or not) to everyone who would listen. As she was gifted in Bible teaching, Nancy took over the weekly women's meeting, through an interpreter at first but soon in her stumbling Maasai, assisted by pictures to help the women know what she was saying. She also gladly helped with the children's Bible clubs. We were often amused that her Maasai vocabulary was mainly biblical, whereas mine was mainly medical and functional. After language study she took over the bookkeeping from me. Nancy also accepted responsibility for the housekeeping side of things, making sure that the mamas did their jobs and had all they needed for those jobs, and that the children had everything necessary for school. Keeping eighty children kitted out with named uniforms and covered schoolbooks, not to mention toothbrushes, toothpaste and shoe cleaning equipment, was a job in itself.

Prayer pact

Thankfully, before we realised how very different we were, we made a pact to pray together every night whatever happened. That was to be the saving of our relationship. I remember reading in a book on missionary relationships something along these lines: 'In our home countries, if you don't like the way Sue eats celery, you don't have to eat celery with Sue. But if you live and work with Sue, and she's the only person you can communicate with properly within a hundred miles, and celery is the only food, you have to learn to live with the way Sue eats celery.'

Nancy saw life in glorious technicolor and was a great storyteller, exaggerating the good as well as the bad, while I played everything down, spoiling all her hilarious stories by insisting on unembellished facts. We knew Satan was attacking our relationship and recognised the problems that could cause, for how could we teach children about a loving God and the unity of the Spirit if we didn't get on together. Jesus himself had prayed to his Father for us: 'My prayer is not for them alone. I pray also for those who will believe in me through their message. ... May they be brought to complete unity to let the world know that you sent me and have loved them even as you have loved me' (John 17: 20, 23). It wasn't just a case of Nancy and I getting on well in order that we could have a peaceful life, if life at Kajiado could ever have been described as peaceful! It was much more serious than that. It didn't bear thinking about that a child whom the Lord had entrusted to our care, or perhaps a visitor to the Centre, could be turned away from God by what they had seen in our lives and relationships. All our Bible teaching would be wasted if our lives denied what our voices said. So every night we prayed together, sometimes through gritted teeth, but we did pray and by the end of that first year the Lord had given us a love for, and an appreciation of, each other – warts and all! Apart from anything else we had a huge workload, and even fingers that squash a louse have to work in unison.

Famine!

A few months after Nancy's arrival the rains failed, the livestock began to die and Kenya was plunged into famine. We bought sacks of milk powder and distributed it to the families we knew had undernourished toddlers. This usually happened when the mother had a new baby and the breast was given to the newborn leaving the toddler with nothing. It soon became obvious that we were just chipping away at the edge of a massive tragedy as the famine spread to all of the Horn of Africa. People despaired. Men were seen desperately trying to keep their cows on their feet long enough to walk them to the slaughterhouse so that they would get a little bit of money for the animal. The stench of death was everywhere as dead and decaying carcasses littered the countryside.

Friends in A.M.R.E.F. (African Medical and Research Foundation) Robbie and Rosemary, headed up the famine relief programme. They organised the transportation and distribution of maize, not only to ourselves, but also to other church groups in the

Kajiado area. The Maasai diet is mainly milk, so their digestive tracts couldn't cope with eating whole maize. Robbie and Rosemary saw to the grinding of hundreds of sacks of maize. Nancy and I were allocated enough food for 200 families based on an average of five children per family. We chose three distribution points, one church building at Sajuloni and two other churches under trees in Eiti and Emarti. First of all, the under fives in each area had to be weighed and measured. The babies were no problem; we hung the scales over a branch of a tree, put the child in a pair of little pants and hung them on to the scales. Trying to persuade the older ones to stand on the scales was a real problem; they just pulled their knees up, screamed and wouldn't put their feet down. The only way to succeed was to bribe each one with a sweet. When we found a very undernourished under-five, based on a ratio of weight to height, we registered the whole family to receive food. We couldn't feed one when the whole family was hungry.

The maize meal, milk powder and sugar had to be mixed together to make sure it was made into nourishing porridge for the children. Unmixed it would have been a temptation to use the ground maize for brewing beer. Not only that, but the powdered milk and sugar would have gone into the grannies' much loved tea. When mixed it could only be made into enriched porridge for everyone. The addition of the three litres of oil we gave increased the calorie content. It was hard to turn people away who didn't qualify for food because everyone was desperate. The resources were finite, but the need seemed infinite. All the church groups in the Kajiado area gave out food on the same day of the week to prevent people registering in two, or even three, different areas. Once a month, as well as the food distribution, all the under-fives had to be measured and weighed all over again to assess their progress. These days were really draining. On one such day Nancy and I were so exhausted that we could only face boiled egg and toast for supper. Nancy said grace, 'Lord, thank you for this food, and please give us the strength to chew!'

Out of all the families in our area we found twelve wee toddlers who were nearly dying from malnutrition and they were admitted to the Child Care Centre. Most of them had reddish hair and a potbelly, sure signs of protein deficiency. To start with they had no energy to swallow or cry. But our housemothers had infinite patience and fed them little by little. As time went on they were collectively known as the choir, because if one of them started yelling the others all joined in. It was wonderful to see their wee personalities emerging and it was even wonderful when they had the energy to cry and be naughty sometimes! For several months they were fed large mugs of nourishing porridge and then returned to their homes in full health. Thankfully we didn't lose even one of our starving toddlers.

Rain!
After ten months the rains came at last, which was great for the tribes that grew food crops. But for the Maasai help was still far off. They keep livestock to

provide them with milk, meat and for bartering to buy food. That meant they had to wait until the few remaining animals had recovered sufficiently from malnutrition to bear calves. Only then did they have home-produced food again. In fact, the rains made things even worse for the people in our area as the river beds, usually dry, were flooded and muddy roads prevented vehicles getting to the people waiting for their food. Also, with the rain came armyworm, thousands of caterpillars advanced eating every blade of new green grass that sprouted. The armyworm was followed by a plague of locusts to finish the job. After that, whenever I saw new little blades of grass I felt guilty even putting my foot on the ground!

When we stopped receiving famine relief food for the local people we started nursery school feeding programmes, which encouraged the younger children to come to school thereby ensuring that they all had at least one big mug of nourishing porridge every day. Nancy also started an income-generating beadwork project with her women's group. She bought beads and leather and had the women make attractive key rings that we sold in Nairobi and to our many visitors. It was tough keeping up a sellable standard of work, and marketing was difficult, but it was good to see women earn cash to feed their families.

By the end of the famine both Nancy and I were really tired. I was due my month's annual leave and decided to take it back in the U.K., to get right away from everything. That was a mistake. The day before I left Kajiado I received a message to go quickly to the village where Anna, who washed our children's clothes, lived. Her daughter's baby had fallen ill during the night. The infant was just a month old. Realising that the message wouldn't reach me in time, fifteen-year-old Mopian started walking across country to the hospital. The baby died in his young mother's arms and she turned back home. I met her there and sat with her as the men dug the grave. Mopian held her dead baby, sobbing, while an old woman shaved its head and then the young mother laid the baby in the tiny grave and we all prayed together. As I sat there I was very conscious of how little the people around me had of this world's goods and how bleakly hard their lives were.

Within two days I was in Edinburgh at Festival time. As I passed through the shopping area on my way out of the railway station I was surrounded by shops selling trinkets for tourists, and passed barrows of little toy animals with tartan bows round their necks; things that were totally irrelevant to life. I was gripped by fury. Tears just poured down my cheeks at life's shocking inequalities. It just wasn't fair.

Nancy

Nancy's great gift was Bible teaching, and after eight years in the Child Care Centre she left to concentrate on full-time Bible teaching to women in the villages. She also had a very fruitful ministry teaching boys who herded calves and goats all day, every day. They learnt to read, to memorise verses from the Bible and heard about Jesus and his love. Several years later Nancy's time of missionary service came to a sudden and unexpected end. One day we received a radio message saying that she had had an accident and asking me to go to Nairobi to be with her in hospital. Nancy had been at a borehole filling water containers on the back of her pickup. The man operating the borehole was meant to turn the water on and off as required. When Nancy finished filling her drums, she shouted to the man in the pump house to turn the water off. Instead of doing that he turned it further on by mistake. The increased pressure caused the hose to snake and, in her effort to control it, Nancy fell backwards. The tailgate of the pickup caught her behind the knees and she fell right over, landing headfirst on concrete.

It was several hours before Nancy arrived deeply unconscious in Nairobi hospital. By then she hadn't just the initial injury, but severe secondary brain damage caused by swelling. Eventually she was flown by Red Cross Air Ambulance to Capetown where she had really good care. After two months Nancy regained consciousness and, with a good rehabilitation programme, she was taught to stand and walk with a walking frame. Her speech cleared and she learnt to read and write again. Sadly the area of her brain dealing with initiative was damaged beyond recovery. Her short-term memory had also gone although her long-term memory remained very good indeed. She even remembered the Maasai language. It was a real joy and sadness to Nancy's friends that she was able, fifteen months after her accident and escorted by Lorna and Betty, to return to Kenya to say goodbye. Having already said goodbye to Lorna, Betty and Nancy for what I thought would be the final time, it was wonderful to return from home assignment two months early and be their driver on that trip and then escort them down to Cape Town for Christmas.

Nancy's Day of 'Well Done!'
By Lorna Eglin

All who love and serve our Lord look forward to that day when, by his grace alone, we hear those wonderful words, 'Well done, good and faithful servant.' On 17th November, at Sajiloni, Nancy had a glorious foretaste of this, as more than two hundred of her friends and spiritual children gathered to praise God for her life and work amongst them.

The service eventually started, more than an hour later than the carefully planned printed programme predicted. Excited recognitions and loving greetings were more important than timetables! Joyous Maasai chorus-singing set the tone as people arrived, greeted and eventually settled down to the purpose of the meeting: worshipping God and praising him for his grace towards us, centring on his loan of Nancy to that community.

The actual church service, scheduled for ninety minutes, lasted for more than double the time, but was well salted with 'choirs' from the various churches (one, impromptu, when we summoned all those with white hair to come and praise God with us). Abie was not the cause of the lengthy service as he gave a brief, relevant, challenging sermon on the need, not only to have a strong faith, but to live it out consistently in life and service.

Then came the speeches! The two minutes limit, grudgingly extended to three, was gloriously ignored. Love and appreciation poured out of speaker after speaker as they gave tribute to Nancy's life and ministry among them. ... Tribute was paid to Nancy's identification with Maasai life, extending to sleeping on their cow-skin beds and tackling hard mielies with her 'shop teeth'. Appreciation was expressed for her humble service – cooking for teaching seminars, transporting goods and people for conferences and gladly meeting whatever need arose.

Nancy's considerable gift for teaching was recognised. Whether in the Scripture classes in several primary schools in the area, or Bible teaching in the churches and women's groups, the Lord has used her to give to many a strong, clear, Bible-based understanding of Christian beliefs and behaviour.

Betty and I were amused (and blessed) as we were repeatedly referred to as the 'aged grandmothers' who first took the gospel into the area. They had heard of us visiting their villages before they were born, or when they were too young to remember. Anyway, as these 'legends of the past', we were encouraged, after the struggles and often discouraging attempts at seed planting of thirty plus years ago, to see the vibrant church leadership of the present day.

Nancy looked like a Christmas tree by the time many had expressed their love and appreciation in kind. Georgie Orme, our dear friend who has worked with disabled children for many years, was presented with a very special gift. A live goat was dragged into the arena by a beautiful young Maasai lady, expressing her appreciation for having treatment and eventual wholeness in the Child Care Centre at Kajiado, as a child. Georgie is coming back to spend Christmas and New Year with us. We trust we won't find her goat amongst the mountain of luggage we'll have on the plane!

For months past Nancy has dreaded this closure, fearing her reaction, being reluctant for the parting. Our gracious Lord answered the prayers of many of you. Throughout, she was wide-awake, with a beaming smile and shining eyes, enjoying it all. She gave her farewell speech with confidence and all were deeply moved.

In the speeches to Nancy there was no empty flattery, only sincere and well-deserved appreciation. All glory was given to God alone. May he be praised!

8
Progress in rehabilitation

As the number of children with polio increased, so did the hours needed each day to stretch their contracted tendons. One day Dr Dick Bransford, a general surgeon from the U.S.A. working at Kijabe Hospital, came on a casual visit to the Child Care Centre. He had no experience of orthopaedic surgery but he just fell in love with the children. His interest in them, and concern for them, was to be a major turning point in our quest for help with rehabilitation. Dick came down to Kajiado each month bringing anyone he could find whom he thought could be of assistance. He did a clinic, and any children who he felt able to help were loaded into his car and taken off to Kijabe. Because the boys and girls all loved him to bits they went happily. It seemed like a great adventure.

Dick learned the simple surgical technique of

nicking a contracted tendon and stretching it under general anaesthetic and then applying a plaster cast to keep the limb straight. The child could walk immediately with the support of the cast and then, when it was removed after six weeks, his leg could be put straight into a caliper. What had previously taken weeks and weeks of passive stretching now happened in minutes. It made a huge difference to the time it took for children to achieve mobility, and much less pain for them and less trauma for me!

So committed did Dick Bransford become to the work that he took every opportunity of learning further orthopaedic techniques, even building up his expertise while on home assignment. On a visit to the U.S.A. he met Dr Stan Topple, an orthopaedic surgeon, and his dermatologist wife Mia, both of whom had worked with the Presbyterian Church for twenty years in South Korea establishing the Wilson Leprosy Centre and Polio Rehabilitation Hospital. After training people to head up the work there they retired to the U.S.A.. Dick discovered that Stan was due to come to Kenya to lecture at a medical and dental conference and also to climb Mount Kilimanjaro. Stan was persuaded to visit Kijabe Hospital and the Kajiado Child Care Centre. He said later that he found seeing the unmet needs heartrending, as many of the deformities could easily have been improved by surgery and/or physiotherapy. The fact that relatively simple procedures could make the difference between dependence and independence made more of an impression on him than either the conference or Mount Kilimanjaro. Dick and Stan stayed in touch; the relationship between these two men was born and nurtured through their mutual compassion for the physically disabled and their desire to serve God and bring honour to his name.

When the doctors in the Wilson Hospital in South Korea heard of the unmet needs in Kenya they were concerned. Dr Kim came to Kijabe in 1988 to help with forty-four children in the Child Care Centre identified by Stan as needing corrective surgery. This strained Kijabe Hospital resources to the limit. Beds were put up in the hospital chapel and I nursed them by day and Dick slept with them at night, hoping to get enough sleep to keep him going through the following day. As soon as the children were able to return to Kajiado they were put in the Land Rover and taken back. My home was turned into a temporary hospital where the boys and girls were cared for until they were well enough to join their friends in the dormitories.

The Korean Christians felt led to extend their helpfulness even further by inviting Dick Bransford to go on a training visit to learn the technique of tendon transfer surgery. I too went to Korea some time later to learn to assess which children would benefit from that surgery. I also studied the preoperative and postoperative physiotherapy requirements. Daniel, my Maasai colleague who was responsible for the Kajiado children's walking aids, was invited to accompany me to learn how to make calipers that could bend at the knee. The trip to Korea was amazing. We arrived in Seoul too late for our onward flight to Yosu and were put up in the Hilton Hotel for the night! Straight from Maasailand to the Hilton! Daniel took the luxury more in his stride than I did.

When we arrived at the Wilson Leprosy and Polio Rehabilitation Hospital we were shown round and then taken to the guesthouse. Our food was served in the hospital canteen – raw fish and kim chi for every meal! I love fish, but the Maasai usually refuse to touch it, putting eating fish in the same category as eating snakes. Daniel, having no choice, persevered, even getting to quite like it. The first morning I woke up at 4.30 a.m. to the tune of *Auld Lang Syne*. For a moment I wondered where I was! But I soon found out that it was a hymn tune, the call to prayer. I went to the church, which was full of people who had gathered to pray for over an hour. This happened every morning and we realised why the church in South Korea is so strong.

I spent most of my time learning all that I could in the physiotherapy department and theatre, and Daniel spent his in the workshop. No one spoke English. Daniel had had three months training in orthotics in Tanzania and this helped him greatly because he knew roughly what Mr Choi, who was in charge of the workshop, was trying to teach him. They used much more basic methods than in Tanzania. Rather than making a full-length plaster cast of an affected limb, they placed the leg on a piece of brown paper, drew an outline, took measurements at various points and then worked from that. This was very much more our style. We could at least afford brown paper! The next step was to bend the metal sidebars, pre-made in a variety of lengths, to the shape of the outline of the leg before attaching leather straps at the necessary places.

Because Korean people traditionally remove their

shoes when they enter a house, the calipers there were attached to a light leather in-shoe that went inside an ordinary shoe. The outer shoe could then safely be removed with the patient still having the use of the caliper inside the house. We could immediately see the great benefit of this for our children as they would no longer need polio boots with straps round the ankles to hold their calipers in place. They would be able to use normal shoes because the little leather in-shoes would hold their calipers firmly.

The tendon transfer surgery made a tremendous difference to many of our children, especially those who needed their knees or hips stabilised. If the muscle that bent the knee was strong enough, the tendon could be brought to the front and inserted into the kneecap. Then, with a lot of work, the muscle that used to bend the knee could be re-educated to straighten it. Also a tail of the abdominal muscle could be inserted into the top of the femur so that when the child lay flat on the floor and raised her head and shoulders off the ground, the abdominal muscles would tighten, and with them the tail going to the thigh bone; thus swinging the leg out. We had special varnished boards made which were gradually tilted as the muscle grew stronger and stronger. The aim was for the child to be able to abduct the leg completely against gravity meaning that the hip was stable. After a month in plaster the children had to exercise for seven hours a day for the first three weeks and then three hours daily for six months to a year depending on progress. It was a huge commitment for both the children and those of us who cared for them, but the results were quite remarkable. After stabilising the knee, the child could walk without a caliper on that leg. And with the hip stabilised they no longer needed crutches. Progress indeed!

A sense of urgency

It was at that time that God brought Joanne Goode to us, just when we needed her most. She came under the A.I.M. volunteer programme. We had to set up my little house again to care for the children who were in plaster and she took turn about with me sleeping with them, as well as supervising all the many hours of exercises. Just transporting all the children back to Kajiado was a challenge in itself. We put boards across the seats in the back of the Land Rover and laid the children head to tail, praying for all of the two-and-a-half-hour drive that no one would need the toilet and that we wouldn't have a puncture. They didn't, thankfully, and neither did we have any punctures on these occasions.

Because polio was virtually eradicated in Kajiado district by the late 1980s, we didn't have new children

Kajiado girls working at their exercises.

presenting with the same problems, consequently we had a specific group who could be helped by surgery. This gave a sense of urgency, especially as we tried to have all the surgery finished during the children's primary schooling. We worked really hard to achieve the goal of having everyone as mobile and independent of aids and appliances as possible by the time they entered secondary school. The children were usually fifteen or sixteen years old by this time because they had started school late.

Babu who was born without feet

Two new children were to highlight another need and challenge. Takaru had crawled into the fire when she was a baby and had lost both feet to gangrene. Babu was born without

Babu with his below-knee protheses

feet and without fingers. It proved impossible to get artificial feet made in Kenya and, whereas a child could walk with crutches if only one foot was missing, both missing meant they had to crawl. Takaru had been helped in Tanzania, but it wasn't possible to rely long-term on services available across the border. Daniel was invited back to South Korea by himself to learn how to make below-knee prostheses. He returned with the technique and some materials to start him off and was able to fit both Takaru and Babu with basic artificial limbs. What a great day that was! In the grounds at Kajiado we had a big climbing frame with a

Takaru with her mother and Daniel. Takaru was the first to be fitted with below-knee protheses

slide and monkey bars. The day Takaru was fitted with her new feet I was in the office doing bookkeeping. She climbed up, slid down, ran round, climbed up again, slid down and ran round, over and over again in utter delight, watching each time to make sure I saw her! I don't know whose delight was greater – hers or mine!

Stan Topple had by then decided that the Lord was calling him to work in Kenya. With a population of twenty-three million people, Kenya had only twelve or thirteen orthopaedic surgeons and only a few of them were engaged in rehabilitation, and of those who were most worked privately. So much of Africa was overwhelmed by urgent medical and surgical needs, especially after road accidents, that disabled children never made it to the top of the waiting list. The Topples came to Kenya to work in the Presbyterian Church of East Africa (P.C.E.A.) Kikuyu Hospital just outside Nairobi. In their respective hospitals Stan and Dick cooperated to meet as many of the needs of the disabled in Kenya as they could. As time passed Stan felt the way opening to propose establishing a Christ-centred rehabilitation hospital with a clear spiritual integrity where patients could be helped physically, while at the same time being introduced to the Lord. He also saw the need for a training programme for doctors, therapists, ortho-technologists and other medical personnel, carried on in a compassionate, competent setting, believing that the fruit of such a ministry would extend far beyond the walls of the Centre.

Very few facilities like the Child Care Centre existed at that time. The Salvation Army had a primary and secondary school and a vocational training centre for the disabled, and the Roman Catholics had a small number of homes. Only a few places were making calipers and none had reached the stage of making artificial limbs. Stan and Dick looked at various possible sites for the new hospital, but the only people who showed any real interest were the Presbyterians who offered land behind the existing P.C.E.A. Kikuyu Hospital. Funding was provided mostly through U.S. Aid and the hospital was built. While it was being constructed Doctor Murila, a fine Kenyan surgeon, underwent further specialist training in orthopaedic surgery and when the new hospital was opened in July 1995 he was appointed medical director and senior orthopaedic surgeon. Stan's vision was the same as ours, that Kenyans should take over any work established by missionaries. About that time land was also given at Kijabe and Dick Bransford established another rehabilitation centre there. Kenya then had two hospital units dedicated to the rehabilitation of disabled children.

We all felt it was a privilege to be part of the process that brought a measure a physical restoration and dignity and a feeling of worth to children who were, at best, little more than an embarrassment in a society where physical performance was so important.

A.I.C. CHILD CARE CENTRE

November 1991

Dear Friends,

Every time I try to concentrate on writing this letter my eyes are drawn to the slide just outside the office door and I am full of praise to God. Little Takaru climbs up time after time, slides down and lands with perfect balance at the bottom. She then looks round to see if I am still watching and then <u>runs</u> back to the steps, climbs up and slides down yet again. This simple act is the culmination of six years of battling to get this wee girl two artificial feet. She had both feet amputated after crawling into the fire as a baby. I never thought that seeing a child running, climbing steps and sliding down a slide could give me such pleasure and satisfaction.

It was the battle we had, and ultimate failure to get Takaru her artificial feet, that made Daniel and I realise we were going to have to work towards making these in our own workshop. As you know, Daniel went back to South Korea for two months in 1990 to learn this skill. It was a whole year after that before the machines he needed arrived; but still the battle was not over – one of the machines needed three-phase electricity and we only had single phase. Joanne battled the whole time I was in the U.K. to get three-phase installed and, wonderfully, just before she left, it was connected up. So our prosthetics department is now open and functioning! Just last week another wee eighteen-month-old boy was brought in, having been born with both feet missing. That makes three children with no feet, and four with one foot missing to give us a thrill each time we see them walking.

Thank you for your continued fellowship in prayer. I do appreciate it.

Georgie Orme

9
Companionship, confidence and courage

From Joanne Jowett (née Goode)

The views from the road leading from Nairobi to Kajiado were everything I had imagined Africa would be like. Driving on a tarmac road out of the city did come as a surprise to me but as soon as we reached the stretch of road that took us through the Athi plains not far south of Nairobi, I knew I was really in Kenya. My first images of Maasailand were of a dry, parched landscape coloured only by the occasional Maasai herder accompanied by a small group of cattle, or the sight of a group of Thompson's gazelle gently gracing the roadside, timidly retreating from the noise of passing cars and trucks.

Having been welcomed into the country by Nancy McElroy, one of Georgie's closest colleagues, the journey to Kajiado which followed was surprisingly fun and entertaining and I soon lost the sense of having to be on my best behaviour! I came to discover that Nancy's sense of humour meant that one could always guarantee having a good laugh when she was around. I had the feeling that, despite my fears about being in Africa, I might just enjoy my time with these missionaries I had never met, and about whom I had heard only snippets of information. With a mixture of nervousness and positive anticipation I approached the Child Care Centre for the first time, escorted by Nancy and greeted at the door of the house by Georgie.

Like many people, I had developed my own preconceived ideas about missionaries and missionary life. For me, it made the thought of becoming one nothing more than a far-fetched idea. It therefore came as something of a surprise to me when God first challenged me about going to Africa, especially since it was the last place on earth I wanted to go. It was a difficult journey for me to get from the place where I was trying to ignore God's voice by putting my fingers in my ears and la-la-la-ing a very loud tune to the point where I could say, 'OK, Lord, if I must!' The 'Please don't send me to Africa' prayer eventually became, 'If you can use me, Lord, I'm ready and willing to go.' Mind you, I think to use the word 'willing' might be stretching it a bit.

Little did I know what an impact this first visit to Maasailand in Kenya would have on me. It certainly was a shock to the system – with life-changing repercussions. It would be a gross understatement to say that those first two months back in 1988 turned my life upside-down. Not only would I be well and truly bitten by the 'Africa bug', about which so many of the great continent-lovers wax lyrical, but I was to form one of the most meaningful friendships of my life.

It was hard for me to conceive how I could be of any real use as a nineteen-year-old with limited life skills and experience, and yet somehow, from the word 'go', Georgie made sure that I was useful. She had confessed to me that she had been reluctant to let me come, having had one or two less than positive experiences with short-term volunteers. In some ways I felt as though I had a lot to prove - a self-inflicted feeling and not one imposed by Georgie. Whilst initially I felt in a slightly precarious position, she entrusted me with an important task right at the beginning which gave me a real sense of being there for a reason.

Companionship
The 1988 visit had been the biggest adventure of my life till then. The six weeks seemed too short a time to really get to know each other, particularly with a thirty-odd year age gap between us. But I had a real sense of Georgie having taken me under her wing and we quickly built up a strong bond of friendship. The whole experience had been a steep learning curve for me but she had been a great teacher. Very long hours of post-surgery exercises with the children, the many cultural insights I gained spending time with Maasai friends in nearby villages, the times of prayer and Bible study, and the many funny moments we shared made for a truly unique experience. Having a seasoned missionary walk with me through those initial adjustments and culture shocks put me in a very privileged position. Georgie was opening up for me what I look back on as one of the most significant periods of spiritual growth in my life. That first visit ended with a two-day trip to Amboseli National Park at the foot of

Mount Kilimanjaro – a treat that was a kind gesture on Georgie's part. We prayed that the clouds would clear so that I could take in my first view of the great mountain. It was a special moment that we shared as that prayer was answered. Poignantly, as the clouds folded back and opened up a breath-taking view, a whole new chapter was about to open for me and for Georgie. I knew in my heart I would be back.

Confidence

Just over a year passed between my departure after my first visit and my arrival for my second term of service. I was to be working alongside Georgie for a year, a period which was later extended to become almost two and a half years. During that in-between year in the U.K., I found it hard to focus on anything else. I knew God was calling me back there but had little idea of what was really in store for me. The prospect of working alongside Georgie again excited me. Our relationship had got off to a great start and we'd had an opportunity to consolidate the friendship when Georgie came to my family home the previous December.

On my first visit I had seen myself as more of an observer, even though Georgie had facilitated a very hands-on approach. This time it was for real. I was a short-term missionary with a very specific role marked out for me. Nancy had already left for home leave in South Africa and I was to replace her until her return. This meant Georgie taking on aspects of Nancy's administrative role whilst handing over some of her usual duties to me. My primary responsibilities included overseeing the hospital transfers for all the kids who were undergoing surgery and then following through with the post-surgery exercise programme. At least twice a week I did Bible teaching, both with the kids at the Child Care Centre and at Eiti School, with the nursery children, as well as taking C.R.E. [Christian Religious Education] lessons with slightly older children. I have many happy memories of teaching God's Word to these Maasai children, gathered under the canopy of a large thorn tree, accompanied by the ring of cattle bells from nearby herds.

Joanne teaching a nursery school under a tree.

At weekends the experience was similar as we would travel out to the children's homes, many of them located in remote areas of Maasailand. On more than one occasion we had to cut a track through the bush to create access to a village for our four-wheel-drive vehicle and to minimise the difficulties for a truck-load of kids with crutches and calipers. Those visits were so special. What a privilege to sit inside little cow dung, smoke-filled Maasai houses, nurturing relationships with such gracious, hospitable people. The sour milk and boiled goat meat might have been a bit hard for my weak western stomach to take sometimes but I couldn't get enough of Maasai hospitality. I watched and learned from Georgie about how to relate to these people and before too long she sent me off on visits without her. That was another test of my confidence but it really stretched my cultural learning and language acquisition.

A goat would usually be killed in honour of our visit and while it was being prepared we would have a service under a tree and share the gospel through the teaching of God's Word and the children's singing with those gathered there. What a sound they made and what a testimony they presented! When news of these visits spread around, people from other villages would turn up for the occasion, some having walked several miles. I have many precious memories of these moments of insight into a culture so far removed from my own and yet with people not so unlike me in many other ways.

With the passage of time, a bigger picture was emerging. Georgie was over-due some home leave, Nancy was returning to a different ministry, and there was a sense that the time was coming for aspects of the Child Care Centre's ministry to be handed over. The A.I.M. office approved an extension on my term of service and this allowed Georgie to take six months in the U.K. It was hard to imagine how I would cope in her absence with around eighty disabled children in my care, even with the support of excellent staff and the Management Committee. But it was a courageous decision on Georgie's part to leave me in charge. During that time, I was joined by an older lady, Irene Walker, who was to take care of the bookkeeping. She was also going to spend time with John ole Kirrinkai to initiate him into the administrative side of the work which Georgie would hand over to him on her return. This would be significant progress in the process of the Child Care Centre being Maasai-run.

My duties were to be more or less the same with the additional responsibility of the medical/clinical side. I was comforted to know that our doctors and surgeons would make occasional visits to help, advise and train me where necessary. I had already taken over all the hospital trips, including the admissions and discharges, so that Georgie could be freed up to do other things. And because I knew I wasn't going to be around long-term it made sense to teach someone else to drive. Marius and John both made valiant attempts under my instruction, but not to the point of passing their tests. Personally, I blame the teacher! Mumeita, however, showed a natural flare at an early stage. After some initial instruction from me and a few professional lessons, he passed his test and became the Child Care Centre driver. This meant that Daniel, our caliper and prosthetics expert, could take over the hospital trips, which later helped pave the way for Georgie to hand over the leadership of the Child Care Centre to him. During her absence we made some strategic advances in the workshop. Daniel had not been able to put his prosthetics training to full use without the proper machinery. Consequently, I spent several months visiting government offices and battling through red tape and bureaucracy in order to get the necessary papers to have the machinery we had ordered released from customs. Added to this was the problem of getting a whole new electricity supply connected to the Centre in order to run the machinery. That was a worse nightmare, but we saw it happen and it was wonderful to be able to walk into the workshop with Georgie on her return to view the prosthetics machinery up and running.

At different times I was called upon to be a nurse, doctor, physiotherapist, administrator, teacher, preacher, pastor, decision-maker and project manager, among other things – for none of which I was properly trained.

They were all things that Georgie had to be, except she was trained for some of them. I was stretched in every direction: professionally, emotionally and spiritually, and sometimes beyond myself. God's supernatural gifting came into operation on so many occasions. I was continually having to 'get out of the boat' and do things that were far beyond my natural capabilities. But looking back I wouldn't have missed a single moment and I'm grateful that Georgie was willing to let me fly, even if there was a risk that I would come crashing at any moment. I grew so much as a person, both in confidence and in my dependence on God. That's one of the great dichotomies of the Christian life. We know that we can do all things through Christ who strengthens us, giving us great confidence, but we also know that our confidence can only be in God, because without him we're nothing. That's a lesson I'm still learning.

As a Christian leader still in my thirties I have shared with many friends and work associates about the idea of mentors. Many younger leaders today have had very negative experiences of working with older leaders who, instead of releasing them to grow, develop their gifts and ideas and allow them to lead, have squashed and stifled them, leaving many disillusioned with Christian ministry. There seem to be so few who are willing to be mentors for a younger generation of leaders, people who can walk alongside them, releasing them to grow and realise their full potential in God. Not many ministry leaders would be prepared to entrust a twenty-two year old with so much responsibility. Georgie did that and I'm grateful to this day. By her unassuming and patient example she nurtured me and walked with me on my spiritual journey.

I have often likened my relationship with Georgie to that of Paul and Timothy, even though we rarely recognised it as such to each other. Her trust and confidence in me spoke volumes and provided the key to unlocking so much undiscovered potential. I don't say this to boast about what I've achieved, but to thank God for the 'Paul' God gave me to encourage me to 'fan into flames the spiritual gift' that was in me.

Courage

Georgie knows what it is to face hardship and spiritual battle head on. Before I first met her, I had heard about some of the things she had faced and it didn't make a life in mission look all that attractive from where I stood. But I admired her strength and fortitude and knew I would have lessons to learn from this. If I'd known what spiritual battles Georgie and I were going to face together, I'd have run a mile in the opposite direction. But we were to learn much of the Lord and from each other through them.

The reality of the spiritual battle dawned just six weeks before my return to Kenya. I was in the throes of preparations for what would be at least a year overseas when I found myself in the intensive care unit of Coleraine Hospital in Northern Ireland having been rescued from a drowning accident in which one of the friends I was with had drowned. It was a struggle to come to terms with the fact that Guy drowned trying to save my life. The enormity of what had happened didn't really hit me until I arrived in Kenya. Georgie later told me that I recounted the story as if it had happened to someone else. But just over a week into my new life in Kenya, I fell apart. I knew I could easily give up and go home, that my friends and family would understand. But God had already prepared the way for me coming out the other side of that experience. Georgie spent hours with me, allowing her shoulder to become wet with my tears. Her silence, her prayers and words of comfort and the example of the courage she'd shown through her own trials in turn gave me the courage I needed to get through the trauma. She helped me face the reality that God's purposes, although not clearly understood, had brought me to the place where I was. I had a responsibility to move forward into God's future purposes, and besides, she wasn't ready to send me home just yet.

'Lord, I don't know if I can do this,' was a prayer I often prayed throughout my time at Kajiado. But in the words of the singer, Ronan Keating, 'Life is a rollercoaster – you've just got to ride it,' (at the risk of sounding tongue-in-cheek). I know that ultimately God's strength enabled me not just to get through, but to thrive in that situation. My last few days at Kajiado were particularly memorable because of the record number of tissues I got through. It was a heart-breaking departure and, yes, there were a lot of tears. Saying goodbye to such amazing children was hard, and my memory of the first time they greeted me Maasai-style with all their wee bowed heads will not easily be erased. Probably one of the most thrilling events was when thirteen children trusted the Lord for the first time at my last Bible club. I was truly overwhelmed by God on that occasion. It was also going to be hard to imagine not having Georgie around. She had shown me true companionship, taught me to be courageous in the face of difficulty and given me space to allow my confidence to grow. I had learned all of these things from *my wonderful parents, but my time at Kajiado took that learning to another dimension and many of the lessons I learned during that time I'm having to relearn now.*

The journey from Kajiado took me to Bible College for three years of preparation for future service. God hasn't taken me back to long-term service in Africa, but he has placed me in roles where I'm engaged in mobilising others for service across his world. Now, as co-leader of Christian Vocations, I still look back to my time in Kenya as being the foundation of everything else that has followed. Of course, life has been full of new and exciting experiences since then, but I thank God for one of the richest, deepest and most unique experiences of my life.

10
Keeping the vision clear

Lengete was one of the early children to come into the Child Care Centre. He had pulmonary tuberculosis and was admitted with his mother to the TB ward in Kajiado District Hospital for a month of daily streptomycin injections before being discharged and prescribed eighteen months of oral medication. Their home was far into the bush, which made it hard for his mother to come to Kajiado each month to collect his medication. When she came to us asking for help we admitted him to the Centre. Poor wee Lengete was so weak he couldn't stand and he wasn't remotely interested in trying. I found a baby walker in Nairobi and sat him in that. Gradually he grasped the idea of how to use his feet to push himself around and, little by little, helped by good nourishing food, he grew stronger.

During the many months Lengete was in the Centre his father came to visit him regularly, usually a little drunk. While he had a real problem with alcohol, he enjoyed chatting to the men who came for Bible teaching in the Evangelists Training Centre. They witnessed faithfully to him and one day he accepted Jesus as his Saviour. Soon afterwards, with the Lord's help, he was released from his addiction to alcohol. Menye Lengete then joined the men in the Evangelists Training Centre classes and soaked up the Word of God. He was thrilled by its teaching and relevance to his life. As there was no church in his home area of Emarti he decided to start one. The family chose a shady acacia tree, and on Christmas Day we were invited to help plant benches under the tree. Holes were dug deep in the ground and wooden posts literally planted into the holes as uprights. Flat pieces of wood were then fixed on top of the posts to make benches – the pews of an open-air church! The church planting was celebrated, after a lengthy service, by big mugs of milk, sugar and tea leaves all boiled up together, and huge hunks of bread. As we praised God together for the birth of Jesus, I thought back to the wee scrap who had been admitted to the Child Care Centre two years earlier and marvelled at what God had done through him. I prayed that He would continue to use our Centre to help to extend His kingdom in Maasailand.

As the number of children in the Child Care Centre increased so did our opportunities of grounding them in God's Word and reaching out to their families with the gospel. The Maasai believe in God as creator. In their folklore he is called 'Enkai'. I realised one day how confident and secure they are in their belief that they are Enkai's special favourite people, and central to his creation, when I received a postcard of a pipe band marching along Princes Street in Edinburgh. The pipers were resplendent in Scottish national dress, each in a bright red Royal Stewart tartan kilt with a plaid over his shoulder. Ng'oto Samuel stared at the postcard for a long time with a puzzled look on her face before asking, 'Who are these men dressed up as Maasai?'

Maasai people love the story of the time long ago when Enkai had a long leather strap stretching from heaven to earth down which he sent his blessings, which were mainly cows for the Maasai. Unfortunately someone, not a Maasai, angered Enkai who cut the strap and severed the path to heaven and withdrew from man. The blessing ceased but they continued to believe they were Enkai's favourites. How like the Bible truth that it was man's disobedience that broke fellowship with our maker.

God is seen as knowing our daily actions. If a child does something wrong at home, he is told, *Keiba Enkai*, 'God doesn't like that.' So they have a sense of God being interested in, and judging, their day-to-day behaviour. They pray often, starting early in the morning when the Maasai women start the morning milking. They take the first milk and splash it up towards the morning star, praying as they do so, 'God who gives us life, care for us today. Give health to our children and grass to our cattle.' These and many other traditional rites and practices point to the true God, who alone can give health and grass. But their beliefs hold no offer of life after death. The Maasai believe that physical death is the end; they won't even say the name of people after they die. And they don't give a baby a name for the first year of life because so many babies die young and their names would then have to be taboo to the family.

The following story is passed down from father to child to teach that it wasn't Enkai's plan that humans die. It was all man's fault.

Once, long ago, at the beginning of time there was a man called Leeyio. Enkai loved him and wanted him to live forever. One day Enkai came to him and said, 'The very next time anyone dies, go outside into the night. Look up at the moon and say, 'Moon die and stay away. Man die and come back to life again.' If you say this, you will never see the light of the moon again, but man will live forever. One day a child of a poor neighbour died and Leeyio remembered Enkai's words. He went out into the night and gazed up at the moon. The moon was beautiful. It gave light to see in the dark. He wondered how they could ever do without the light of the moon. How would they see at night? How would they see the wild animals that came to attack their cattle? He thought, 'That child who died isn't very important.' So he twisted Enkai's words and said, 'Man die and stay away. Moon die and come back again.' Suddenly he heard wailing from inside his own village. His own son had died, his firstborn, and his favourite! In deep grief he lifted the body, carried it outside the village, and looked at the moon in desperation and, remembering Enkai's words, said, 'Moon die and stay away. Man die and come back to life again.' But it was too late; Leeyio had lost Enkai's offer of life by his disobedience.

So Maasai children are taught not to blame God for death. Death came because of man's disobedience. Enkai had wanted to give man eternal life, but it was lost because Leeyio disobeyed him. We could easily explain to the children that that story is different from the one in the Bible, but the result was the same. Adam and Eve disobeyed God and because of their disobedience death came into the world. It was even better to be able to tell them that death isn't the end. There is a way back to God because Jesus, God's Son, came into the world as a man. He died on the cross in our place, to take the punishment for man's disobedience, and that by believing in him we can have eternal life.

A joyful day

The New Testament was first translated into Maasai in the 1920s but had long been out of print. It was many years before a revision was finished, but what a great day of celebration it was when the first box of bright red-covered books arrived at Kajiado! Those who could read drank in God's Word and rejoiced. However, our enthusiasm was dampened when we discovered how few people could read. Life Ministries, realising the problem, recorded the whole of the New Testament on to cassettes. And Gospel Recordings put out tough hand-wind cassette players so that all, readers and listeners alike, had access to the precious Word of Life in their own familiar language.

Every morning after the children went off to school our housemothers gathered around the kitchen table, with a cassette player in the middle, and listened eagerly to God's Word in Maasai. It was wonderful to see the joy on their faces. Nancy had tried hard to teach them to read but, although they had a great incentive, a combination of age, failing sight and poor concentration made it difficult. As they loved to spread the gospel, we provided each of them with a wind-up tape player and

Housemother with tape player and picture book about creation

tapes. On their days off and holidays the housemothers walked from village to village playing God's Word to anyone who would listen – and most people did, intrigued by how the voice got into the box! Later Gospel Recordings produced a series of eight Maasai language tapes with accompanying illustrated books covering from creation right through to Revelation. These helped tremendously in sharing the message of God's love in far off villages where that gospel wasn't known.

One of the great things about living in such a close community with the children was that it was as if they were growing up in a Christian family. We held Bible clubs for them every week and laid great emphasis on memorising portions of Scripture. Apart from committing the Word of God to memory and, we hoped, into their hearts, it meant that when they went home they could share it with their families. One Christmas I found the nativity story in little books with pop-up pictures. Each week in Bible club the children practised telling the story with the pictures. Then the older ones each went home with a copy of the book to share the Christmas story with their families. Later we found the Easter story and that was used in the same way.

Toes for eyes

While I was away on leave on one occasion Betty and Lorna heard of a badly disabled child and went to visit her home, finding a dear wee girl called Kesene. She was a happy, confident, much-loved child and her parents wondered if there was any help for her. My friends eventually got her to the relevant specialist who

Kesene has arthrogryposis and is blind

identified her trouble. Kesene had arthrogryposis, a congenital condition that resulted in her having webbing of her joints, making it impossible to straighten elbows, knees or hips. She was also blind, born without eyes. Kesene had developed her own style of walking; she waddled with knees and hips bent. The specialist told Lorna and Betty that surgery to straighten her limbs would hinder rather than help her. Boots, calipers and crutches would have been of no help to her either as her toes were her eyes;

her bare feet told her where she was. Kesene's toes

Kesene, who cannot see, being led
by a friend who could not walk

followed the edge of the path. When my colleagues took the wee girl to the Child Care Centre she was at home at once, bouncing on the first sprung bed she had ever met and enjoying the new clothes in which Ng'oto Samuel dressed her. But when she demanded shoes it made them all, including Kesene herself, very sad.

When I returned from leave I found Kesene well established in the Centre. Ng'oto Samuel had gently led her in the ways of God and she was deeply responsive to Jesus; she loved Him. God gifted her with a lovely singing voice and the ability to compose Maasai songs like this one that became a great favourite:

> *I know in my heart, you are a good God;*
> *You made Turere's toes straight because you are*
> *a good God.*
> *You made Nchaa's back strong because you are*
> *a good God.*
> *You healed Naishorua because you are a good*
> *God.*

This song went on and on with a verse about everyone in the Centre!

Kesene had a great desire that everyone who

came to us at Kajiado should know her God. One day I was showing some visitors around, *wazungu*, white people. I found it easy to talk to Africans about the Lord, but somehow with white people I often felt that they might think I was trying to push religion down their throats. So I was hesitant in telling them about all the wonderful things that God had done in the Child Care Centre. On this occasion I was telling the visitor, 'This is the kitchen. This is the workshop, where Daniel makes the calipers. Here is the hydrotherapy pool …,' when I felt a little tug at my skirt. I looked down and there was Kesene. 'Ask him if he loves Jesus,' she said anxiously in Maasai. The visitor looked at me, waiting for me to translate what she had said. I swallowed hard and said, 'She wants to know if you love Jesus.' The visitor gulped with embarrassment and answered, 'I was brought up to worship God, but since I married I have never been inside a church. But coming here today has really made me think.' Whatever wonderful things God may have done in that man's life, it wasn't due to me. I would never, to my shame, have asked that question. Thank you, Lord, for your special children!

Every Sunday a group went to lead a service at one of the children's villages. We took someone to preach and a number of children to sing. Whoever's village it was had the privilege of choosing which children would go on the trip, often more than two hours driving in each direction. I just loved getting out into the Maasai villages. They were so peaceful in comparison to the bustle of Kajiado. The low houses, made by women from a woven framework of sticks smeared with cow dung, were very dark and smoky;

smoky because there was always a fire smouldering, dark because there was just one 'window' to let smoke out and light in. But the window was often stuffed up with a cloth to keep the snakes out! Maasai people are very hospitable. We were always invited into a home while 'chai' was made for us on the open fire in the centre of the house. In times of plenty we would be given great big mugs of sour milk to drink. Their extra milk was stored in huge gourds and shaken every day until it was the consistency of yoghurt. The taste was lovely and smoky because the inside of the gourd was first smoked with burning slivers of olive wood.

Rejoicing in flies

The houses were divided into compartments, with two or three alcove beds made of brushwood and each covered by a cow-skin, where everybody cuddled up together to sleep. There was also an alcove for the baby animals to be warm and safe at night. I loved the gentle lowing of the cattle and the tinkle of cowbells, but not the air-splitting bray of the donkeys! The clouds of flies swarming over everything were actually associated with blessing. No flies means no cow dung. No cow dung means no cows. No cows means hunger, poverty and disaster. So they endure and rejoice in the flies!

The children loved to stroke my skin and feel my hair. One day a wee girl plucked up the courage to stroke my hair. She turned to a friend and said in great amazement, 'She feels just like a cow!' Coming from people who esteem their cows so highly, I took that to be the ultimate in compliments!

On special occasions our arrival at a village caused a bustle of activity and someone would be sent off to choose a goat for our meal, and we hoped the goat was pastured not too far distant! Some women would head off with their pangas (large, very sharp multi-purpose knives) for firewood, and others carrying cans for water. We could have a lengthy service, with many choirs and testimonies, because our lunch was still several hours away! Eventually the goat would be slaughtered and skinned, part stewed and some roasted. We ate the meat with huge mounds of rice and needed no supper when we arrived home. No wonder going to church in a village took all of Sunday!

Church wasn't quite what might be expected. Everyone from the village and around was summoned to the service. 'Come, we've a message for you from God!' we told those who didn't know what was going on. The woman and children gathered round eagerly, all sitting on the ground to hear what God was going to say to them, while the men stood quite a distance away. If a man decided to stay, he would summon a child to bring a wooden stool for him to sit on. It is beneath a man's dignity to sit on the ground. And men wouldn't be seen gathering with women and children but they would sit near enough to see any pictures we had brought and to hear what was being said. Our wee choir of children always sang and the older ones were encouraged to tell how God had helped them and what he meant to them. On one such occasion Kesene said, 'Until I came to the Child Care Centre I didn't know that God had a son called Jesus or that he loves children. Now I know him, and I know he loves me. I don't have eyes in my body, but in my heart I see Jesus!'

Every year the children performed a nativity play in the big Africa Inland Church in the compound. They practised for weeks and found suitable dressing-up garments in the clothes store. All the teachers from the nearby schools were invited and also everyone who worked in the District Commissioner's office. On one memorable occasion a star was rigged up on a pulley going the length of the church. The wise men hobbled on their crutches slowly up the aisle following the star, which was being pulled to where Mary and Joseph and the baby were at the front of the church. There was great consternation when the star stuck. The wise men didn't quite know what to do. Eventually someone clambered up and freed the star and the wise men were able to continue on their journey. When they reached the manger, they knelt down to worship Jesus and present their gifts. Oseur, who had paralysis of both arms and one leg, having knelt couldn't get up again! Everyone laughed but I had a big lump in my throat,

It became a tradition that the party following the nativity play was organised by the children who were leaving to go on to secondary school or vocational training. It was a lovely surprise when the first group to leave did this, completely of their own initiative. Someone got a goat from home and they collected money for the rest of the food from their families and the other children. After many speeches each member of staff was given a small present to say thank you for all their care.

One weekend a team of preachers we didn't know came to take services in the town. Unknown to me the team claimed to have a healing ministry. I was safely in bed when they decided to hold a late night service in our church. The children were invited to go, and among those who went was Mundeli.

'Anyone who has enough faith can be healed,' the children were told. Mundeli, who couldn't stand without her crutches, wanted to be healed.

'Do you believe you are healed?' she was asked.

'Yes!' the girl replied confidently. Her crutches were taken away and she fell to the ground.

'Just keep believing and you'll be able to walk,' Mundeli was told.

Another girl, who was bed-bound and had been carried to church that night, was told that if she had enough faith she'd be able to get out of her bed in the morning. The next morning all the children ran to her bed to see this happening, fully believing it would. She just lay there looking at them, unable to do any more than before.

I can only guess what affect that experience had on the children, but it certainly affected me. I was so angry! It seemed so lacking in wisdom and discernment and sensitivity. I could do nothing other than pray and leave the whole situation with the Lord. Over the years I had always tried to protect the children's tender faith. Might I sometimes have quenched the work of the Holy Spirit? But how cruel to make promises to disabled children and shake their precious faith in Jesus and his love for them.

Complete healing!

I was especially grateful that in Bible Club the children loved learning about heaven. They really could relate to the words in Revelation chapter 21:4, 'He will wipe every tear from their eyes. There will be no more death or mourning or crying or pain, for the old order of things has passed away.' No more hospital trips, no more pain, no more operations, no more blind children and NEW bodies! Freedom from all disabilities! Complete healing! What a wonderful thing to look forward to.

Eventually Ng'oto Samuel, who had such a tremendous influence on the children, had to retire. Even at the most generous guess she was well past the Kenya government retirement age. Having been diagnosed with cancer of the thyroid gland, she required surgery and would be on medication for the rest of her life. After about a year of retirement she arrived back one day to say, 'God has been so good to me. I feel he is calling me to come back to the Child Care Centre to serve him. I don't want any pay; I just want to stay and teach the children.' About the same time we heard of an operation that was being performed on children with brittle bone disease. The long bones were broken and a metal rod inserted to straighten and strengthen them. We called Shomet back and he had surgery on both legs. By then he was really a man, but as he was child-size he still fitted into the Child Care Centre. After surgery, because Shomet desperately wanted to stay on at his old home, he teamed up with Ng'oto Samuel and they formed a little pastoral care team. Together they led prayers with the children each evening and had time to sit and talk to them as individuals which, sadly, because of our busyness we didn't always manage.

We needed to constantly remind ourselves to keep our vision clear. The ministry of the Centre was to bring children to faith in the Lord Jesus Christ. The children had to be fed, with all that was involved in food buying. They had to have their medicines and have their wounds dressed. They had to have physiotherapy and be taken to hospital. They had to be educated, with all the work that was involved in keeping them in school and training. The workshop had to run, including many trips round the industrial area to get supplies. Keeping the Centre going was a huge operation also involving bookkeeping and communication with sponsors. In the early days especially, time for preparation for Bible teaching was the thing that got squeezed out. It was a constant tension. I praise God for Ng'oto Samuel, now in heaven, and Shomet, who completed a course in tailoring and is now happily married with a baby of his own. God gave them the vision to minister the love of Jesus to the children and they were obedient to his calling.

Shomet, now a tailor, is married with a child

A.I.C. CHILD CARE CENTRE
November 1989
Dear Friends, I've just asked Joanne, 'Why is it that my mind always goes blank when I sit down to write

a newsletter? I can't think of a single thing that's happened.' She replied, *'Well, I can't think of a single thing that hasn't happened! That sums up life at Kajiado pretty well!*

Since I last wrote we've been out quite a bit in the villages. First there was the circumcision ceremony of one of our older boys where, sadly, according to custom, a lot of beer had been brewed and most of the men were very drunk. I realised afresh how hard it can be for our children when they go home – Parsalunye and his mother are the only Christians in that village. Please pray for the children at home during December.

Just after Joanne came we were invited to the ceremony where junior elders graduate to be senior elders. There were 192 huts in a huge circular **manyatta**. We spent the day going round chatting to the people I knew, drinking tea, eating meat and watching all the festivities. The unity all the men of the age-grade share was demonstrated by their wives all hammering a stake into the hide of the ceremonial bull to pin it to the ground and then later the men all sat in a huge circle and each ate some meat from that same animal.

One Sunday we went with Daniel and his wife and children to their home village two hours' drive from here. One of Daniel's brothers has now become a Christian and he and Daniel's mother have started a new wee church under a tree. They had invited quite a few visitors, many of whom had not heard the gospel before. After the service we had a meal together and then I left a wind-up tape player and the Maasai New Testament on tape with them. Do pray for this new little group that more may come to know the Lord. Pray also for more effective use of the tape ministry.

A few years ago I tried to supply some people in the villages with tape players and the Scriptures, but I grew discouraged because the tape players are expensive and break quite easily. Also the tapes themselves often fall into the hands of children who enjoy pulling the tape out to see how long it is! Now there are many more tapes available in Maasai, some of which go along with pictures of Bible stories. This would be a really good way of helping Christians who can't read to learn, and also a good way to help them spread the gospel. So pray that we can find a way to overcome the problems.

Another thing that concerns me is that we have far less contact with some of the children's villages than we used to. In the early days, William and I taught in all the villages at least once a term. Now there are many more children and much more work. This also means that there are more opportunities for outreach but less time to take them up. I would like to see an evangelist working with us, concentrating especially on the contacts made through the Child Care Centre, and I wonder if this could be combined with supervising the tape ministry. This would also require a driver as some of the villages are very far away. Last week I took Marias, who rides our message bicycle, for his first driving lesson. But as we careered across the plains at about fifty m.p.h. in second gear, with his foot glued to the accelerator and every word of Maasai I'd ever known deserting me, I realised that my nerve was not what it once was, and that I was not the one to teach him! So please pray for this whole project and all that it involves.

Thank you for your prayers.

Yours aye,

Georgie

11
Lessons and life
experience shared

'In all the many miles I drive in remote places I have never been completely stranded.' This was my testimony on many occasions as God had always made sure there was someone to help when I needed it. On one occasion a Maasai warrior used his spear to break off the stuck padlock holding the spare wheel when Nancy and I had a puncture in the middle of Amboseli Game Park. Often I arrived home safely and then a tyre went flat at the front door. The opportunities for disaster were many, but the Lord had always sent help until one day when he had a big lesson to teach me. I was driving along a corrugated road, taking a child home to Loitokitok on the northern foothills of Kilimanjaro. I had a visitor from the U.K., and I was looking forward to sharing the beautiful drive with her and the buffalo, elephant and many kinds of gazelle that grazed on the open plains, with Kilimanjaro as a glorious backdrop.

Suddenly I saw a wheel overtake me and veer off into the bush. It was only as the car ground to a halt and fell to one side that I realised it was my wheel I had seen! All the wheel nuts had sheared off completely. After rescuing the wheel, the three of us sat at the side of the road wondering what to do. There was no public transport on that road, only tour buses. We sat for several hours like birds in the wilderness. Eventually a tour bus came along and gave me a lift back to Namanga leaving my visitor and the child with the car. I managed to find a mechanic and we hired a vehicle to take us to the car. As soon as he looked at the wheel he said, 'Your wheel nuts must not have been on tight enough and the metal has cracked with all the corrugations on the road.' While he drilled the remaining bits of wheel nuts out and fixed the wheel on I had plenty of time for reflection.

The previous day the car had a puncture on the way home from Nairobi. I changed the wheel and was just tightening the nuts when a man came along on a bicycle.

'Can I help you?' he asked.

'No thank you. I have finished,' I replied. Showing off to my visitor who was listening to the conversation, I said, 'It's always the same when I have a puncture. I finish changing the wheel and then a man comes along, tightens the wheel nuts and looks like he's done all the work!'

As I watched the mechanic fixing the wheel on to the car it was as if the Lord said to me, 'Men are stronger than women. Next time you have a puncture and I send you a man to tighten the wheel nuts, just say "Thank you!"' The mechanic tailed us on the rough road back to Namanga and then we limped slowly, wheel held on by nuts and bolts, back to Kajiado. I know the visitor enjoyed her adventure. It made a good story, but I have never forgotten the lesson!

Another big lesson was how to give help wisely! Water was always a huge problem. Our water was piped fifty miles from artesian wells in the Ngong hills on the outskirts of Nairobi. Maasai herdsman often hacked into the pipe to get water for their cattle and we were left dry. Lorna and Betty had a strict rule that we never gave water except once a week on the day of the women's meeting. Each woman was allowed to bring one twenty litre container to fill with water. We often had people desperately searching for water and when it was in short supply everyone was under pressure. I found it so hard to say 'no' when we had some. Surely if we gave freely to everyone the Lord would honour that and give us more, I reasoned. When at last I had my own house with my own water tank I felt I was free to do what I believed to be right. Lorna and Betty were away, and I was expecting a family of four, on holiday from Scotland, for lunch. While I was preparing lunch the first person came looking for water and I gave some. Within a few minutes someone else came, then another and another. Swarms of people from every direction came over the horizon, each carrying their empty jerry cans. I gave freely and gave and gave and gave....

By the time the visitors arrived I had not a drop of water left. Still people were coming from every direction. The word had got round, 'Naado is giving water.' 'I have no water left,' I said to the next lot of people who came. I could see in their faces that they didn't believe me. My confidence that the Lord would honour my generosity was fading fast. Then the Child Care Centre ran out of water. The housemothers, knowing I had a full tank, came to get some for the children. 'I have no water left!' They were incredulous. 'How could you finish a whole tank of water in a morning?'

When I told Ng'oto Samuel I had given all my water away, I was in big trouble.

'Kokoo and Ng'oto Ntoyie said we must only give on women's meetings day.'

I tried to explain why I had given my water away.

Ng'oto Samuel said patiently, 'When people come, tell them we need our water for the children. Tell them the children can't carry their own water and we can't carry water for forty people. They will understand'.

We ended up having to pay for a water tanker to bring water and I learned a huge lesson. Don't take God's provision for granted and be wise, remembering those depending on me. My visitors left highly embarrassed that they couldn't even flush the toilet. They continued on their tour of Kenya, but they never forgot their visit to Kajiado!

Misplaced faith

I wish I could say I never again took the Lord's provision for granted. God supplied us so abundantly that it was easy sometimes, without even realising it, to take it for granted.

There was a time when we were so short of money that we had to decide which bills to pay and which we could safely leave. Our subsidy from C.B.M. for salaries and food was held up. We had to discontinue building a staff house. The promised help to fix the solar heating in the hydrotherapy pool didn't materialise and it was too cold for the children to use. My car needed repair, as did my typewriter and the photocopier. The Centre's Land Cruiser had two completely bald tyres. The promised cheques for secondary school fees for sponsored children didn't arrive. A change in the administration of my work funds meant there was no money to cover Bible School fees for Stanley, a partially sighted boy, or for Peter, a disabled boy, both of whom we were supporting. Every day it seemed there were new and urgent needs: a hearing aid for a wee boy in a local school, food on a regular basis for a family of seven desperately undernourished children whose parents were both profoundly deaf. Then the news came that Daniel's wife Lydia needed open-heart surgery which couldn't be done in Kenya. Where on earth would all that money come from? I felt quite overwhelmed.

In desperation, one morning as I was praying, I said, 'Lord why are you allowing all this? What are you saying?' My devotions that morning were in James 4. Verse 2 ends, 'You do not have, because you do not ask God.' At once I realised it was true. Over the previous months I had gradually fallen into the trap of looking to donors and organisations for our needs instead of to the Lord. After confessing that and asking his forgiveness I went over to staff prayers and shared what the Lord had shown me. We then spent a long time in praise for all God had done, and in prayer, earnestly bringing all our various needs before him.

Imagine the rejoicing the very next morning when a truck from a solar heating firm drew up at our door with all the equipment not just to fix, but to completely renew the pool heating system! Then came the post with two letters and notification of a registered letter awaiting collection. One letter had a cheque to be used for 'something that will benefit you' – repairing the typewriter and photocopier. How could I manage without them for typing and duplicating my weekly Bible study notes for the children and also for preparing my newsletters? There was even enough to have the car fixed. In the other letter was notification of a gift to replenish my general work funds depleted by Lydia's hospital investigations, enough to pay Stanley and Peter's college fees and to buy a hearing aid. The registered letter contained the cheques for the secondary school fees. And the next day I had a telephone call from the British High Commission telling me of twenty boxes of clothes and shoes that were about to be delivered along with a gift of money for new tyres for the Land Cruiser.

It was as if the Lord had put everything on hold until I acknowledged afresh that everything we are and have comes from him. And more was to come – a gift of £1,000 for Lydia's heart surgery from a lady who had undergone open heart surgery herself. It was God's promise of what was to follow. It would be two years before God brought the people into our lives who would coordinate Lydia's care in Northern Ireland.

Many others gave financially, British Airways allowed her to travel free, and Daniel for half fare, while both surgeon and anaesthetist gave their services without charge. Only the hospital bed had to be paid for. When Lydia returned into the care of her cardiologist in Nairobi he said, 'God really loves you, Lydia. The heart valves you've been given are the best available.' God's hand was very clearly on Lydia from the moment the problem presented itself until she returned home looking better than she had done for years.

Daniel escorted Lydia and stayed with her while she had the surgery. That was his third visit to the United Kingdom, the first en route from South Korea when he and I went there together. I took Daniel round some of the A.I.M. prayer groups in Scotland and Northern Ireland in order that he could share some of his life experience with the people there. He gave his testimony, and it was wonderful to hear him getting to the point of realising that it was through being disabled that he had come to know the Lord. Everywhere we went Daniel asked people to pray for his family because none of them were believers. When we arrived home

Daniel and his mother and brother with a tape player and New Testament tape.

we discovered that his mother had become a Christian! Before long Daniel's brother became interested and he and his mother listened to Scripture tapes on a wind-up tape player we gave them. Prayers were answered in a wonderful way as others came to the Lord. Daniel's brother learned to read, and eventually led a little church that was planted under a tree at their village.

Mombasa ... here we come!
Although disability was the norm in the Child Care Centre, when our children went away to school they often felt left out. This was most obvious when school trips were being arranged. Often these involved too much walking for even the most mobile of our boys and girls. I had enjoyed many visits to Mombasa over the years and longed to share the experience with the older children. So it was decided that I would take the two senior classes of boys one year and the girls the next. Their joy at least trebled mine! For them it was an adventure they had never dreamed they would have, for me it was a wonderful climax to over nine years of work. While God had worked many miracles and supplied everything we had needed over the years, as I drove from Kajiado to Mombasa I never dreamed he would be such a fantastic tour operator.

The drive was long and cramped and grew progressively hotter as we dropped from almost 6,000 feet to sea level. But as the temperature rose, so did the level of excitement. Can you remember your first glimpse of the sea? The boys just about jumped out of the windows with excitement! Mombasa town is on an island. You drive over a causeway to get on to the island and then north over the Nyali Bridge to get off the island again.

'Slow down! Slow down!' they all shouted, as we drove over the bridge because they could hardly take in that we were driving all that distance above water. I was so enthused at their enthusiasm I forgot about the cars behind us until I heard the loud hooting from people who probably crossed the bridge every day and wanted to go faster than five miles an hour!

When we reached Kanamai Christian Holiday Centre I immediately led the boys to the beach and found hardly a drop of water our side of the reef. I was so disappointed as I had imagined us jumping straight into the water; but God had the timing all worked out. After a picnic lunch we were able to walk all over the sand almost out to the reef, which was normally covered with water at high tide. This let the boys see little fish and shells and crabs in rock pools and reassured them there wasn't anything too terrible under the water when the tide did come in. Maasai men have the reputation of being very brave, but our would-be warriors didn't do too well when confronted with their first sea slug! When we did go swimming I was ready with large rubber rings and yards of rope to tie them together, my imagination full of pictures of the boys floating across the Indian Ocean to Mumbai. All this proved totally unnecessary as the sea was so calm and no deeper than waist height. The boys just loved the water as they were so free, devoid of the heavy metal calipers and boots that were normally so much a part of their lives.

The Lord opened up door after door for us, even allowing a visit to the old port of Mombasa which can usually only be visited by prior arrangement. When I went to ask for permission I discovered a sign in the office reading, 'Jesus is in charge of this office.' He was! We were shown round by an official who really understood boys and knew exactly what they would enjoy seeing. What a thrilling hour we had being shown Arab dhows all made from wood, some from Lamu, being loaded without the use of machinery as they have been for over 200 years. He showed us all the different departments: customs, health and immigration. At the end of their wonderful visit, the official said, 'Boys, the most important thing in your life is to trust God. I have trusted him since I was a boy, and he has helped me get to the job I have now, in charge of this port.'

On the Sunday we went to church at the Word of Life compound south of Mombasa. This involved driving the car on to a ferry to cross the Kilindini Channel. More excitement! We had been praying for Word of Life for some time, since meeting Stanley, a partially sighted young man who joined us each Sunday evening at Kajiado for a meal and a time of Bible teaching by tape. Stanley, like many other young people in Kenya, had been brought to the Lord and spiritually matured through the ministry of Word of Life camps, and I wanted our boys to be introduced to this too. On the way home that day we had a sail in a glass-bottomed boat. The sailor knew exactly where there would be coral and fish; he had even brought bread for the boys to feed to the fish. For over two hours ten faces were glued to the long glass panel in the floor of the boat, shrieking in delight at everything that moved. I am quite sure that the boatman had never had a more excited or satisfied group of customers!

Another highlight was the visit to Bombalulu, a workshop where disabled people were trained in a wide variety of crafts, mostly making things for the tourist trade. The boys were particularly impressed by the woodwork section. There was a young man who had been trained in carpentry and given a room and a loan to help buy materials and set up a business. After six months he hadn't only paid back his loan, but was able to employ another four disabled men. This young man made a tremendous impression on our boys. With both legs in calipers, and supported by crutches, he talked to them for a long time, impressing on them that however great their disability, if they were prepared to work hard and trust God, they would be able to succeed. Bombalulu would also be a success with the girls the following year. After finishing secondary schooling Jemima, a beautiful girl, became receptionist there and a model for their clothing and jewellery, even featuring on an Air Kenya brochure. Years later she was given an award for services to the disabled in Kenya.

Jemima modelling Bombelulu clothing

On the last morning of the boys' trip we were up bright and very early to allow time for one last visit before heading home. The boys wanted to see the new port, but when we asked for permission to do so we were not even allowed to park the car. I pled to talk to the man in charge, telling them where we were from. Just then the man himself came out of his office and said, 'Let these people in, I have a special interest in this group.' Turning to me he said, 'My father is the pastor of Loitokitok A.I.C.,' one of our churches in the Kajiado district! Not only did our boys see ships and cranes and forklift trucks, they were taken aboard a relief ship – down to the engine room, up to the bridge and they even held the ship's wheel. They were so excited!

As we headed back to Kajiado on the long eight-hour journey I thought of these boys when I first knew them, crawling around in dust and cow dung, covered with scabies. I reflected on all the pain from surgery and physiotherapy, the years of being hampered by calipers and crutches and not being able to run and jump as most boys could. They had even been denied the possibility of showing their bravery, as others of their age group in Maasai culture were required to do. I thought of the determination they had shown over the years and I knew that, in my eyes at least, there were never any braver Maasai warriors than these ten boys.

FROM WILSON REHABILITATION FOUNDATION
RECOGNITION AWARD PRESENTATION
26th APRIL 2002
SPEECH BY DANIEL M. OLE SAPAYIA

Ladies and Gentlemen,
If I told you I am happy that I am disabled some of you would probably say, 'This little cripple has gone crazy.' But if you had lived with me, you would understand. In order therefore for you to be part of this understanding,

I beg to indulge you with a bit of my past history – the experiences that have moulded me.

My mother was the first of my father's five wives. Unfortunately for her, although I was her first born, I was my father's third born. Then polio struck me at the tender age of two, at a time when my father was already proudly displaying his son and daughter from his second wife. These two were the joy of his life and he didn't even notice the fate that was befalling his third born, the first born of his first wife. My dear mother therefore became not just the woman that brought me into this world, but she was also my childhood playmate, a friend and soul-mate.

Life is hard and harsh for a child growing up in rural Maasai land. It is miserable and unbearable for a child disadvantaged by physical disability and an unloving father, to grow up in the same environment. My father looked at me as an enigma, a curse upon him from someone. A series of unfortunate events confirmed his fears. Firstly, my mother bore me late after marriage. Being a poliomyelitis victim is not what is expected of the first-born child of his first wife. I was not a normal Maasai child. I didn't look after lambs, sheep, goats, cattle or calves. I didn't have fun playing with other children, running, dancing, wrestling, fighting and hunting. I just crouched and sorrowfully sat with women as a man watching all these activities and other events unfold. My father cursed and ostracized my mother for bearing him this curse – a punishment and reminder of his wrong doing as a warrior.

The direction my future life was to take was brought about by a government directive that all families must send a least one child to school. This was a God-sent opportunity for my father to get rid of me, the same God that toughened Pharaoh's heart in order to reveal his awesome power and set free the children of Israel. With a smile and big relief, my father handed me over to the chief and the second phase of my life began.

My early years at school were like that of other disabled children, painful, emotionally and physically, not being able to play with the rest! Eventually I accepted my disability, helped by the Bible verse where Jesus explained that a man who was born blind was not so because his parents sinned but because God had a purpose. Mine was about to be revealed. After school I joined Kericho Vocational Rehabilitation Centre where I learned the art of shoe-making, and upon completion I set up a tiny Jua-kali shoe-repairing banda in Kajiado town earning enough for food for the rest of the day.

One day God sent his angel in the person of a Mzunga woman for me to repair her shoe. She liked my work and thought that I could be better utilised elsewhere. Georgie Orme of A.I.M. from Scotland took me to A.I.C. Child Care Centre and literally opened the world for me. ... She brought Child Care from a Home Care Centre to an excellent institution with orthopaedic facilities. The technical know-how, training, guidance and advice was provided by a close friend of the Centre, Dr Bransford of Kijabe Medical Centre. Naado, as we call Georgie, realised the need for training. She very generously offered me this. She was determined to build, mould and prepare me psychologically. She became my mentor. In 1986 Naado arranged for me to go to Tanzania for four months training in prosthetics and orthotics.... In furtherance of this training Georgie arranged for me to train as an orthotist /prosthestist in South Korea in 1989/90 at Wilson Rehabilitation Centre....

My life at the Child Care Centre has been a big challenge for me. I've realised my full potential at the

Centre under the guidance of Naado. I now know that my disability was surely a gift from God because it had a purpose. I no longer feel sorry for my disability. I feel blessed! On reflection, I've no doubt in my mind that had I not been disabled, I would have been where all my able-bodied brothers and sisters are, there in the jungle with hunger, diseases and poverty.

A couple of years ago my father was taken ill. His cattle, and those of his able-bodied sons, having been finished because of drought, he was dependent upon me. I was happy and blessed to be the one to offer him that care and love. As a sign of his appreciation, and regret of his earlier mistreatment, he blessed me and put me in charge of his total family before he died. God does work in mysterious ways. I feel I am a role model not just to my family, but also to the young ones, disabled and helpless, over 500 of whom have gone through the Child Care Centre since 1979. . . .

The honour bestowed upon me by this Award is a testimony of the determination of disabled people to be one among equals. That Wilson Rehabilitation Foundation has chosen me for this Award is a great acknowledgement that disabled people can make a change. I therefore wish to dedicate this Award to the Child Care Centre, its Committee and staff, and my wife and family, and all who have made this possible. I now thank you all and wish you God's blessings.

Daniel M Ole Sapayia (slightly edited)

12
Moving on

Lorna and Betty moved north to Kiserian in Baringo District in 1983 and found the people friendly because they knew the local language. Soon after they settled there was a serious drought. The livestock was decimated and 'the grannies on the hill,' as they were called, found themselves involved in a widespread famine relief programme, which helped them to know the wider community and become known by everyone. The work advanced quickly. Relief distribution centres developed into churches, a nursery school and primary schools. Through 'food for work' programmes, classrooms and churches were built. Child sponsorship also funded the building and running of a clinic. A great need was met when they were able to build and administer a secondary boarding school.

Because of my bond with them, whenever they found a physically disabled child they let me know and then invited me to visit them and see the child. I assessed these children and often took them back to Kajiado where they stayed until their surgery and treatment was complete. Two dormitories had been built alongside the primary school in Kiserian for the use of pupils who lived too far away to walk to school daily. These dormitories were ideal for the children who had undergone treatment in Kajiado.

One of these was Helen, who came from a very poor family. She had developed a severe infection in both feet which, after a year in hospital, developed into gangrene and she lost all her toes. When I first saw her she had both feet bound up with filthy old rags and she was loath to remove them even for the doctor. Because the skin on her feet was so fragile and broke down and ulcerated easily she was fitted with boots with special insoles. Helen was still so ashamed of her feet that she wouldn't remove the boots even to get into bed.

When I returned Helen to her village after treatment in Kajiado was complete, a group of men stopped the car. There was obviously something seriously wrong. Helen's father had lost all of his animals in the drought and was desperately depressed because he could no longer feed his family. Shortly before we arrived Helen's father had been found hanging from a tree; he had committed suicide. This already emotionally scarred wee girl suddenly had more to cope with. It was decided the best way to help the family would be to admit Helen to boarding in Kiserian School so that at least she would have food to eat during term time. Two other girls, Maria and Mareton, joined her. They both had paralysis of both legs following polio. Maria, who also had weakness in both arms, had already got as far as standard five in a school for the physically disabled run by the Catholic Church, 100 kilometres from her home. The person who was helping her with transport left and Maria had been unable to continue with her education.

I had no sooner returned to Kajiado, happy to have been able to help these children, when news came that the girls had been sent home. It transpired that the food provided by the government for the boarders had run out. That was no problem for the able-bodied children – they would have a long walk each morning and evening, but it was possible for them to live in their own homes. For Helen, Mareton and Maria it meant the end of their schooling. Concerned for the needs of his physically disabled pupils, Samuel, the headmaster, asked if I could help him create a more stable boarding facility. It wasn't possible at that time as I was due to go on home assignment.

Gradually, Kajiado Child Care Centre had been getting more and more independent under the leadership of the Management Committee. John was in charge of bookkeeping and administration, Anna, housekeeping and child-care and Moses was responsible for building and maintenance. We also had a driver. This meant Daniel was able to take over all the hospital trips with the children, allowing him to be much more involved in their medical care. He enjoyed that and did it all well. When planning for my home assignment, the Management Committee suggested Daniel should be in overall charge in my absence. I knew that if he succeeded in managing the work I shouldn't go back. It was hard to leave as Kajiado had been my home for seventeen years. He did succeed and I knew that my work there was done.

On my return I was given the use of a missionary couple's home in Kiserian as the Kochs were on home assignment. It seemed the ideal opportunity to help Samuel to create the stable boarding unit he needed for his physically disabled pupils. By then there were twelve of them. Where to begin? The local church council held interviews and selected Ng'oto Anna, an older Christian Njemps lady, as housemother, helped later by Joyce. Ng'oto Samuel came out of retirement once again to help me. She worked with Ng'oto Anna, instilling into her how to show the love of Jesus to her young charges.

The long drop toilets were dug on a food-for-work basis. As I had a gift of money to buy maize meal for undernourished children, their fathers worked in return for the food.

Samuel used a donation of school uniforms to get sand and gravel for the concrete slabs. The parents were called to collect the donated uniforms for their children but had to 'pay' with a bucket of sand or gravel. It was a real community effort. Moses, our Kajiado builder, came to help us construct a small kitchen and food store. Within a couple of months we were established and complete with beds, sheets and mosquito nets for the children, all provided with the help of sponsorship of some of the children, by the

Arms of Jesus children's mission in Canada. Samuel was so committed to the education of physically disabled children that he enrolled on an in-service course to study for the Diploma in Special Education.

Famine and then El Niño

I was no sooner settled at Kiserian than famine reared its ugly head again. As there had been no rain for several months it was back to weighing and measuring the under-fives and doing what we could for them and their families. My heart sank as I saw the all too familiar signs of malnutrition wreak havoc among the people, especially the children. Thankfully the affected area was much smaller than the horrendous Horn of Africa famine of 1984-5. A big gift for famine relief through A.I.M. enabled us to buy sacks of maize and milk powder, which Pastor Thomas and I distributed weekly as fairly as we could. The Njemps live around Lake Baringo and fish is a big part of their diet. But when the lake receded due to lack of rain it was impossible for them to get to the water to fish because of all the deep mud. Unfortunately when the longed-for rains came, they came with all the force of El Niño and made life even more difficult. After the drought it seemed to rain non-stop for the whole year I was at Kiserian. When I went there the lake was over a kilometre away from the bottom of the hill where the missionary house, church and dispensary are. By the end of the year the water came right up to the foot of the hill.

To get to Kiserian I had to cross three rivers, two with bridges and the third usually shallow enough to drive through. When the rains were heavy the whole area between the two bridges flooded and I had to make a huge detour to get to Marigat on the main tarmac road. It was on this detour I discovered Lake Bogoria Hotel, complete with spa pool fed from the hot springs of nearby Lake Bogoria. As my joints were sore from driving through all the mud I bathed several times in the spa pool to ease my aches and pains. Little did I know how much time I would spend there in the future.

The people made the most of the rainwater, digging irrigation channels to their gardens and planting maize as soon as they could. What wasn't washed away had plenty of water to encourage growth. Consequently the Njemps recovered from their famine much quicker than the Maasa did, as they only had to wait until the maize grew to get food.

The roads were so muddy, and sometimes underwater, that it was hard to know if you were on a road or not. One night the rain was pouring down so heavily that I had to keep going off into the bush to avoid getting stuck in mud. All that lit the area outside the beam of my headlights were flashes of lightning, and they came often enough to give me some idea where I was. When I eventually arrived back in Kiserian Pastor Thomas was waiting for me. 'O praise the Lord,' he called out in relief. 'I have been praying for you all evening, knowing you would be on the road in that rain.' Pastor Thomas was a dear and fine man who cared for me. It's good to remember that while missionaries care for those they serve, local Christians cherish and care for their missionaries.

My midwifery skills occasionally came in useful during my time at Kiserian. One night I had friends staying with me, and we were all fast asleep in bed when a knock came to my bedroom window. It was the nurse asking me to help with a lady in delayed labour. The baby's head was well and truly stuck and the nearest good maternity unit was a two-and-a-half hour drive away. We put the woman in my car and drove all the way to the hospital expecting her to need a Caesarean section. As soon as the patient was put on the delivery table out popped the baby, probably dislodged by the very long bumpy drive! Amazingly, the baby came out screaming. I asked if I could give the new-born its first spank! By five o'clock in the morning I had returned the mother and her baby to her home and headed back to mine. When I apologised to my friends for the nocturnal disturbance it transpired that they had heard nothing at all. I told the whole story, and when I enthused how amazing it was that we got a live baby, one of my friends, who was more awake than I was by then, looked up at me from his breakfast and said dryly, 'Great! Live baby; dead missionary!'

Nancy

One of the first children helped in the Kiserian boarding unit was Nancy. She came from a very poor family who lived in a traditional Njemps house outside Marigat, a small town near the main tarmac road. Both her parents tried to scratch a living working as casual labourers in the irrigation scheme, where pawpaw, tomatoes and onions were grown mainly for sale down country. When Nancy was very young she contracted polio, which resulted in paralysis of both legs. That was one problem too many for her parents.

Nancy was left sitting in the dust by herself all day. Her older brother, Teemu, was physically disabled due to cerebral palsy. He also was in the boarding unit. When I first took Nancy for surgery to straighten her contracted paralysed legs prior to fitting calipers, it was a great relief to her parents. As the years passed her returns home became more and more difficult; it was a constant struggle to get the balance right between the emotional and physical needs. Nancy always went home looking plump and healthy, but when she was collected for school again after three weeks sitting alone in the village she was thin and withdrawn.

The girl became old enough to sense the reluctance of her parents to welcome her home. She was one more mouth to feed, one more problem. On a memorable occasion, having taken the children to see the flamingos and the hot springs at Lake Bogoria, followed by a visit to the stuffed lion in the hotel lobby, I drove home dropping children off at their villages for the December holiday. Nancy was the last to be delivered and, as she got out of the car, she hung on to the hem of my skirt more and more tightly. Although her parents tried to look welcoming, their rejection hurt her deeply, and it hurt me too. It was a privilege to introduce children like Nancy to the Lord Jesus for he will never reject them. I prayed that she would give her life to him and experience his deep love for her, bringing healing to her body and, more importantly, healing the emotional scars she bore.

Tribal conflict

Intertribal conflict was an ever-present tension between the Njemps and the warlike Pokot tribe, brewing from time to time into fighting and bloodshed. After a long period of drought the Njemps men were preserving an area of grassland on the edge of the lake as emergency grazing for their cattle. The Pokot heard about this and one day brought several hundred head of cattle to graze. The Njemps retaliated by impounding many cows and goats, and the Pokot then brought their guns and fired into several Njemps houses. The women and children fled with the animals, while the men had a council of war. I was called to collect the disabled children from the boarding unit and take them to a safe place.

I bundled all the children into the car not knowing quite where to take them because all their families had run away. Being physically disabled our children couldn't run. Kitiboi was nowhere to be found. A snake had bitten him a few years previously and the resulting scar tissue that formed over his knee contracted and held his knee in a bent position. After several plastic surgeries the knee was straight but the skin was fragile and prone to crack and ulcerate in the hot humid climate. The boy stayed in the boarding unit, where we could keep an eye on him, but he didn't consider himself a child and resented being fussed over.

I searched and searched for Kitiboi. Eventually I went to where the men, warriors and tribal chiefs were having a meeting with officials from the District Commissioner's office, who were trying to cool down the whole conflict. There was Kitiboi, in the middle of the warriors, with his dagger tied round his waist, carrying his bow and arrows. I decided not to embarrass him by insisting he come with the rest of the children and he stayed to fight the Pokot! When peace resumed and school opened again for the end of year exams, Kitiboi turned up safe and sound.

James in his chair made by the Kampi carpenter.

Some parents made a huge effort to find help for their children. Little James was brought to Kiserian by his father, who pushed him twenty-five miles on the back of his bicycle. He had cerebral palsy and couldn't sit up. When people heard that such children were being helped in Kiserian word spread like ripples on a pond. I heard of more and more children who needed help, many of whom were on the other side of the lake. Really all I could do with the children with cerebral palsy was to help parents cope at home. Because people sat mostly on three legged stools, a child who couldn't balance was left lying on the ground. The result of this was that muscles unaffected by their medical problem wasted through lack of use.

A local carpenter used his skills to make a huge difference to these wee ones. I took him to their homes and he measured them and made padded chairs with trays in front and with footrests attached. This got the children up out of the dust. They were so proud of their new chairs! Parents were shown exercises to strengthen the children's neck and back muscles and then encouraged to make parallel bars from metal piping so their children could practise walking. Kandie's mother, a keen Christian, was a nursing orderly at Marigat Health Centre. She did everything we taught her to do, followed every instruction, was diligent with every exercise and her son was living proof of her commitment. Eventually we managed to get a wheelchair for Kandie in order that he could be taken to the local school. The clever boy was first in his class!

Mama taking Kandi to school

What now?

At the end of my year in Kiserian the little boarding unit was going well, and the family whose house I was in was due back. I had another couple of years to work before I planned to retire to be near my mother. Kajiado was doing well under Daniel's leadership and Kiserian was under the supervision of the headmaster. What now? During the year I had made friends with the pastor and his wife in Kampi ya Samaki on the western shore of Lake Baringo. Joseph was a qualified pastor and he and his wife, Anna, were also graduates from the Africa Inland Church Missionary Training College. Kenyan pastors were encouraged to train as missionaries and reach out with the gospel to unreached tribes in their own country and further afield. Joseph and Anna had started the A.I.C. in Kampi ya Samaki.

While I was still praying about what I would do at the end of the year, Anna said to me one day when I was over seeing children at Kampi, 'When the Koch family come back you'll have to find somewhere else to live and I have found the very house for you. You people like quiet, and this house is very quiet.'

Knowing how busy and noisy Kampi always seemed to be I didn't have a lot of confidence that anywhere there could be quiet. But she was so convinced it was the Lord's house for me that I obediently let her lead me there. I was so used to driving through mud by then that I paid little heed to Samuel and Anna's warnings. I ought to have known better as the house belonged to Samuel, who was one of the church elders! It seemed such a small patch of mud in comparison to what I had been tackling all year and I drove confidently into it and the car sank up to its axels! It was a swamp I would get to know well.

We left the car and walked to the house. Ignoring the smell of fish from where the last tenant had smoked his catches, ignoring the filthy walls that had never seen a lick of paint, and ignoring the snakeskin hanging from the corrugated iron roof, I stood completely captivated by the view. I would happily have lived in a tent to have such a beautiful view of Lake Baringo. Another bonus was that as the house was on a cliff a little breeze helped to reduce the number of mosquitos. An arrangement was made that I was to have the house rent free for a year on the understanding I would dig a long drop 'choo,' construct a shower room and build a small veranda, all of which would upgrade the property. I painted it all white, including the outside of the roof to deflect the sun's rays and make the inside less like an oven. It was a dear wee house and I just loved it.

Word continued to spread that someone was coming to Kampi who would help disabled children. After settling down I assessed needs and made arrangements to take those who could benefit from surgery to Nairobi. We had two good rehabilitation hospitals down country. The challenge now was to link up-country disabled village children with these facilities. The logistics were like a military operation. Those who lived north of me came the night before the hospital trip and slept on the church floor, fed by Anna and the other church ladies. Those who lived between the hospital and me were told to be at the side of the road at 6 a.m. ready to be picked up.

Usually my swamp wasn't a problem. It made quite a smooth path most of the time as we had such little rain. One day I left at 6 a.m. in perfectly dry conditions and arrived back at 9 p.m., after a cloudburst, to mud. 'Can't be that bad,' I thought, lulled by tiredness, as I pictured my bed not two minutes away. I had a very disabled girl with me and she too was weary. Once again the car sank up to the axles in mud, the end of a long and difficult day.

That morning I had arranged to pick up several children at the side of the road in order to meet up with Daniel at P.C.E.A. Kikuyu Hospital Rehabilitation Unit just outside Nairobi. One mother and child was missing. After a lengthy search I eventually found her waiting at the wrong road junction! We set off almost two hours late for the four-hour drive. Daniel was already there, having arrived from Kajiado two hours before me. He had seven patients and I had five. He usually helped me get my patients organised, but by the time I arrived he was already totally involved with his own.

Tired and hungry I stood in the queue to register the patients ... then the queue to pay ... back to the end of the queue for registration to prove I had paid. The notes were then sent through to the clinic and we sat in the queue to wait to see the doctor. Daniel appeared briefly at this point and managed to speed things up a bit. Dr Murila admitted three children for surgery: one very disabled child needed a physiotherapy assessment to see if surgery had any hope of getting her mobile; another required an x-ray. So ... back to the queue at accounts to pay for the assessment and x-ray. Then, like Daniel, I tried to be in three places at once: waiting at x-ray, helping with the assessment in physiotherapy and up on the ward with the others for admission. Eventually we found ourselves back in the queue to see the doctor with the x-rays and the assessment. All my patients were admitted and I left the hospital at 4 p.m. with only Dina, whom Daniel had brought up from Kajiado.

Dina was twenty-two years old. She suffered brain damage at birth, had cerebral palsy and walked with a frame. I tried to get her a place in vocational training to do tailoring but she wasn't accepted because she only had five years of primary education. She chattered in Kiswahili all the way back to Baringo. She had a speech impediment and I had a partially deaf left ear. Kiswahili was her second language and my third. I was also dodging buses and trucks on the very busy Nakuru-Nairobi road.

Dina lived way up in the Tugen hills, a great place for training marathon runners but very hard for disabled people. There was no way I could get her home that night, which is why we were sitting together in the mud en route to my house. To cut another very long story short, after three hours and my shoes sucked off in the mud, never to be seen again, we were pushed out backwards. I found lodgings for Dina in town, and someone to stay with her, while I trudged home through the mud in my bare feet.

Having found Dina somewhere to stay overnight, and having lost my shoes in the mud, I arrived home cold, wet, tired and miserable. All I needed was a hot cup of tea. My muddy hands wet the matches so I couldn't light the lamp or put the kettle on. Sitting down on my bed at midnight I reflected on the day. Thundering into my reluctant thoughts came Philippians 4:4, 6-7. 'Rejoice in the Lord always. I will say it again: rejoice! … Do not be anxious about anything, but in everything, by prayer and petition, with thanksgiving, present your requests to God. And the peace of God which transcends all understanding, will guard your hearts and your minds in Christ Jesus.'

I had prayed fervently for rain, and my rainwater tanks were full; how could I be anything less than thankful? Then I thought of all the years of driving disabled people around in all sorts of difficult terrains and hardly ever been completely stuck; this time I had been within sight of home. My spirits lifted and peace returned as I praised the Lord for his provision, protection and help and then collapsed into a very deep sleep.

From PRAYER LETTER

July 1998

'Trust in the Lord with all your heart and lean not on your own understanding; in all your ways acknowledge him and he will direct your paths.'

I remember learning the above verse as a child and have proved it true many times. Why then am I so apprehensive during times of change? Will I make the right decisions? Is this really where the Lord wants me to be? Am I going off on my own tack or is this what he wants me to do? I have to keep reminding myself that the Lord wants me in the centre of his will far, far more than I want to be there; so as long as I trust him and acknowledge him in the decision making, he WILL direct my paths.

Pray that as I move from Kiserian in August over to the other side of Lake Baringo, the Lord will make it very clear which children he wants me to work with. I have been quite overwhelmed by the number of disabled children I have been asked to see in the last few months. Many of them are badly brain-damaged following meningitis. My answer so far has been, 'Wait until August when I'm living on the other side of the lake, I'll have more time to help then.' I've lost count of how many times I've said that and August is coming fast! Pray I will not get so busy with physical needs that I lose the vision of why the Lord has me working with these children and their families.

One of the children I've already tried to help is the daughter of a Pokot evangelist. Reuben and his wife

Esther were married for ten years with no children. Reuben remained faithful to his wife and after ten years the Lord blessed them with three children. It was such a witness of the Lord's faithfulness to the Pokot community where there were few Christians. The third child, a little girl called Chepkite, became ill with meningitis when she was only ten months old. Esther walked for miles to get to a dispensary. It was not equipped to deal with such an ill child so she was referred to another dispensary, and yet another. Imagine the desperation of that mother trying to find medical help for her child. From the history I worked out that it was ten days before Chepkite got proper treatment!

She is now two and a half; she cannot sit or eat and has a tube draining fluid from her brain to keep the pressure down. She cries a lot of the time and is very difficult to feed. Many people have prayed for healing but the Lord has not yet healed her. As I sat with her in the doctor's clinic in Nairobi and during the long car journey back up north and saw the distress of mother and child, I begged the Lord to either heal her or take her to be with him and release her and her family from their suffering. Pray for Reuben and Esther that they will stay faithful to each other and to the Lord.

The missionary who asked me to try to help Chepkite said he really knew there was nothing anyone could do to help, except show we care. And I guess as I look forward to August and all the other brain damaged children I've been asked to see by parents with so much hope, there will be very little I can do except show that I care.

There is another little boy I've seen briefly who has spina bifida which has never been treated. He is paralysed from the waist down, is doubly incontinent and has lost all his toes due to various infections caused by dragging himself along over the stony ground. Paulo is about nine years old and a really sweet child. I managed to get a wheelchair for him from Kajiado but stupidly never asked where his village was. When I arrived I found the village on a flattened out piece of ground perched halfway up a hillside – we had to carry the wheelchair as there was no way of wheeling it! Paulo was thrilled to bits with the chair but he won't be going very far in it! Pray for Paulo and for wisdom for the doctors as I take him for assessment regarding possible treatment in August.

The Lord has provided me with a lovely little house in Kampi ya Samaki. The people have been so welcoming and even planted flowers round the house and have organised someone to carry water for me. The long drop toilet has been dug and a washroom constructed beside it. I went last week to do some painting and hope to build a simple verandah with mosquito screening so that there is somewhere cool to sit. Pray for me as I move in August and begin to make relationships with the people there.

The Lord is so good he gives us all good things to enjoy. My favourite food is fish and Kampi ya Samaki is Swahili for 'the camp of fish'. I don't know who is going to be happier eating tilapia every day – me or my cat!

Sincerely in Christ,

Georgie

13
A jembe, a panga and a cattle prod

I loved my wee home near Kampi ya Samaki despite some unwelcome visitors, namely snakes. My friend Nancy, who was terrified of those creatures, had tried to instil in me a healthy fear of all snakes, even providing me with a *jembe* (a kind of metal hoe) and a *panga* (a long knife) for protection. The idea was that when encountering a snake I should first put on my wellington boots so that it couldn't strike at my ankles and then immobilise the snake with the *jembe* before cutting off its head with the *panga*. I have to admit that I didn't pay much attention to Nancy's detailed description of how to kill a snake as I had never been too troubled by them. I suppose that she, having been brought up in South Africa, knew a good deal more about them than I did. Scotland does not have a large snake population!

I had used Nancy's murderous technique to good effect on several occasions. Two of my victims were identified as black mambas, and I had begun to take heed of the maxim, 'Treat all snakes as highly poisonous until proved otherwise.' But just in case I was bitten by a poisonous snake I had acquired a battery operated cattle prod that gave a substantial electric shock when activated. It was claimed that when used on a snake bite site it rendered the venom less potent. The Kampi ya Samaki area was teeming with snakes because of the heat and the porous volcanic rock.

One evening it was already dark when I returned home from a hospital trip. As I went through the door I froze; there was a snake on the roof beam just above my head. Startled by my sudden appearance it slithered off at high speed and I lost it. Knowing that it was in the house somewhere, I was especially careful about tucking in my mosquito net before settling down to … lie awake all night! The following night I was again late home. I undressed for a shower, which was in a tin hut out the back of the house, and wrapped a long cloth round me. To my horror I saw my visitor lying along a strut under the roofing above my bed. I slid my feet into my wellington boots and grabbed the *panga*. As the snake was above my head the *jembe* was useless. Standing on a wooden stool as far from the creature as I could, I speared it about a foot behind its head and the point of the panga sank into the roof. Unfortunately there was a lot of give in the roof and the snake thrashed around, striking at the *panga* for about twenty minutes before it died. As I held the *panga* in place I shouted out to the Lord for help and then found myself in a fit of giggles. I was suddenly aware of the ridiculousness of my situation. My cloth had fallen to the floor and I stood, completely naked apart from wellington boots, pinning a snake to the roof with a *panga*! When it was all over I hammered the head as hard as I could and cut the creature into bits, each piece still writhing and thrashing. I thanked the Lord for sparing me once again.

About a week later I came into my home and shone a torch around. My coming in startled a snake on the roof and it disappeared through a gap in the wooden struts to the outside of the house. I noted where the gap was and plugged it with foam. The house was well-known for its snake population and the man who owned it advised me that these creatures didn't like moving over oil. The next morning I took his advice and poured a large can of oil all round the house to prevent any more coming in. Having some oil left, I climbed up to pour the remainder round the hole through which the snake had escaped. Unknown to me it was still hiding in a crack in the wall. As I reached to apply the oil the snake darted out and bit the middle finger of my left hand just above the knuckle. My last sighting was it flying past me to I knew not where.

Nancy had told me you only have twenty minutes to live after being bitten by a black mamba. I had flippantly retorted that if I were ever bitten by one I would make myself a cup of tea and sit down and prepare to meet the Lord. I didn't. My survival instinct took over. I applied the cattle prod and gave myself some hefty shocks. That done, I realised I had to get to where there were people. I drove, with one hand, in the direction of the town, not knowing just how long it would be before the snake's venom would begin to take effect. I was driving round a fenced area on my way to our little town when I remembered that someone had mentioned there was a snake farm there and I suddenly realised that might mean help.

Turning into the compound, I told the first person I met that I had been bitten by a snake and, before I realised what was happening, I found myself being cared for by Jonathan Leakey, *the* snake man in Kenya! 'Calm down,' he told me urgently. 'If you get excited your blood circulates more quickly and the venom moves through your system quicker too.' I tried to relax. 'Now,' he said, 'describe the snake to me.' I was able to do that as I had had a good look at it. 'That was a black mamba,' said the expert seriously. 'I have the right anti-venom here,' he explained, 'but it can cause anaphylactic shock, so we need to get you to hospital and administer it there.' Turning to his wife, he told her to phone the hospital in Nakuru, well over a hundred kilometres away, to alert them of our coming. I was bundled into Jonathan Leakey's car and he drove at high speed to the hospital where there was a red alert to try to find anti-venom which was nowhere to be found – they didn't know we were bringing the only anti-venom in the whole area with us. By the time we arrived I was finding breathing difficult and my vision had blurred.

Some years before my encounter with that snake I had attended the Keswick Convention and a speaker began his talk by announcing that Christians were hypocrites. A gasp went round the tent. 'Let me prove it to you,' he said. 'Hands up all those who want to go to heaven.' I think every hand in the tent went up. 'Now, put your hands up if you want to go to heaven right now.' There was a kind of embarrassed giggle before a silence descended. 'You see,' concluded the speaker, 'we say that it would be wonderful to be with God in heaven, but the minute it looks as though we are about to go there we start treating the prospect as a major disaster.' That had made a big impact on me, and I prayed that when my time came to die I wouldn't treat it as a disaster. I asked the Lord to help me to be ready and happy to go to be with him.

As I struggled for breath, that incident at the Keswick Convention came into my mind. 'Right, Lord,' I prayed. 'I'm ready. Just take me to heaven.' Then I thought about my mother. She had buried her son, my dad and my stepfather. My prayer changed. 'Please Lord, let me live for Mum's sake.' All this was spinning around in my mind, I can remember it clearly, but I was far away from what was happening around me. The staff set up ready to intubate me if I collapsed with the anti-venom, but I didn't, and it began to take affect quickly. My breathing gradually relaxed and I thought the worst was over. I suppose it was, but it certainly didn't feel like it.

The snake's fangs were removed from my hand and I was given antibiotics. Despite them I developed a raging infection and found myself in truly awful pain. My whole arm swelled up and my hand was in a terrible state. For five days I remained in hospital before the decision was taken to fly me to Nairobi for surgery. By the time I arrived there I was seriously ill and a surgical team was ready to take me right to theatre. The surgeon thought I was going to lose my hand, but he managed to clean it up and do a skin graft to prevent atrophy of the nerves, blood vessels and ligaments. That saved my hand but more serious grafting techniques were required to make it useable again. A Swedish plastic surgeon working in Nairobi attached the back of my hand to a flap of skin from my groin. I was left with my hand attached to the skin flap in my groin for three weeks until blood vessels, growing across the operation site, fed the graft from the hand itself. When that happened the graft was partially detached and, only when the blood continued to circulate freely, was it fully detached some time later.

The Lord sent the right person to be with me at just the right time. Rosemary Gilmore, from Northern Ireland, who had come out to help me in the work at Kampi ya Samaki for six weeks, became my companion and nurse and we went down to Mombasa to allow me a time of convalescence. I even enjoyed swimming with two plastic bags taped over my hand, which was still heavily bandaged. Rosemary was a great help and stayed with me when I returned to hospital for further surgery. Our Mission authorities had phoned Mum to let her know what had happened, and as soon as I was fit enough I phoned her every day to reassure her that I was on the mend. Some days she seemed quite confused. On the very day I had my final stitches removed there was a phone call to the A.I.M. office to say that Mum had died. It was 31st August 1999, and I had hoped to be back in the U.K. to celebrate her eighty-fifth birthday that October. Instead I found myself, after nearly three months in hospital, back in Darlington for her funeral. I then had to clear her house and sort out her affairs. That was a really hard time; illness and grief both gave me a battering.

A caring church

By the time I returned to Kampi ya Samaki two months later word had spread that I had been bitten by a snake. Everyone also seemed to know that my mother had died. The local people suddenly realised that here was someone needing to be cared for and looked after. Even strangers (though nobody is ever really a stranger in Africa) brought presents and helped me, and from then on I was truly part of that community.

A dream gains substance

Local people were aware of my work and had become more conscious of the problems that disabled people faced. The chief of Kampi ya Samaki area, Patrick Kiror, was a great support. In Kenya chiefs are not hereditary but civil servants chosen by the government. Chief Patrick, who was very much loved

Chief Patrick

and respected, opened many doors of opportunity when he started coming with me out into the country to assess newly discovered disabled youngsters. He was especially determined to accompany me when I went into Pokot country as the people there were armed. When I suggested that he didn't have time to go the long distances with me, Chief Patrick, a gentle and kind man, explained that he was responsible for all the people in his area, including me and those who were disabled.

I had thought of the work in Kampi ya Samaki taking me up to retirement age when I would return to the U.K. to care for my mother, but her death allowed for a complete rethink. As I was contemplating the future and praying for guidance, two things happened. Rosemary asked if she could take a career break from her work with disabled children in Northern Ireland and spend it with me. I was thrilled. Also over £5,000 was given for the work with disabled children in the Baringo area. The door seemed to be opening for me to remain and set up a centre in Kampi ya Samaki like the one in Kajiado. But that had taken seventeen years to establish, and even if I worked beyond retirement age, my health was such that I knew I didn't have many productive years left. With that in mind I approached the local church and explained the situation, telling the elders that if I were to remain to establish a work, they would have to be prepared to take it over in the long term. The men were very enthusiastic about the project and, at my request, formed a Committee to take it forward. That done, I took Chief Patrick, the local pastor and some of the Committee to P.C.E.A. Kikuyu Hospital to see what was being done there, and then on to Kajiado where Daniel introduced them to the work of the Child Care Centre. Inspired and excited by what they had seen, we returned to Kampi ya Samaki to begin a smaller version of the same work, a halfway house where children could be brought and cared for en route to the two good rehabilitation hospitals down-country. Everyone was very enthusiastic. There was a real buzz about the place.

Rosemary's request for a career break met no problems and she was accepted by A.I.M. as a one-year volunteer. She became the main driver of a Toyota Land Cruiser we were given for the work. One of her first jobs was to take the Committee to a quarry to choose stones for the building. The people of the area were very poor and construction methods were basic. The church women earned money to help their families by carrying water for making cement from the lake. One of the elders was a builder and he organised casual workers to help him and also transport of sand and other building materials. The organising Committee embraced their new work with huge enthusiasm. First to be built was a concrete block tank to hold the water the women carried. Then they built a dormitory and kitchen, and these were followed by a workshop and later a second dormitory. Just when it was needed we received a gift of £2,000 to equip the workshop!

While the construction work was proceeding, God was working out his plans in quite another area. Before my encounter with the black mamba, I had met a severely disabled young man called Daniel who dragged himself along the ground wearing flip-flops on his hands to prevent them being damaged. More than anything the lad wanted to be trained in a trade in order to provide for himself. Was there anything I could do? Mercifully there was. Daniel, whose legs were far too bent for corrective treatment, was sent off to do a leatherwork and shoemaking course. In his amazing sovereignty, God was providing a workshop at the same time as the young man who would work there was training for the job! 'Would you be interested in coming to work in Kampi ya Samaki?' When I asked young

Daniel, after I had explained the whole situation to him, he was delighted beyond words! He was given a wheelchair, and in his holidays he went down to Kajiado to be trained in metalwork and the measuring and making of calipers by the other Daniel. When the Centre was ready to be opened, he had finished his training and was prepared to begin work.

Daniel Kangogo in his workshop

Rosemary was due to return to Northern Ireland in the late summer of 2001 and the Committee decided to arrange an opening ceremony before she left. Africans love ceremonies, and this one was to be very special. There were balloons everywhere and the ribbon, which was to be cut by the Regional Church Chairman, was draped across the door of the Centre. The scissors he was to use were placed on a pillow and carried to him on a tray. About 150 people gathered for the celebration and feasted on rice and goat stew. Kajiado Daniel came with a group of staff and 'old boys' for the weekend. One of them, Keswe, who had graduated from Daystar University, said 'Now Kajiado Child Care Centre has a brand new baby to care for!' Several of those who had been helped over the years testified to God's goodness. It was all very moving indeed and really inspired the Kampi ya Samaki people.

A week later Rosemary returned home and, at the beginning of 2002, I left on home assignment. I left knowing the Committee members were keen and wise, that Daniel had been trained, had passed his government trade tests and that Kajiado Daniel would visit on a regular basis. Luka, the treasurer, would look after finances and food buying, while Mama Jane and Mama Ndanyi would care for the children. The practicalities were well worked out. Children were to have their hospital treatment at P.C.E.A. Kikuyu Hospital before going to Kajiado until all their medical appointments were over, their artificial limbs and such like made, and their physiotherapy complete. Then they were to return to Kampi ya Samaki to board while attending school. And while they were there, any work needing done on their calipers and boots would be carried out by young Daniel. God, who knew the end from the beginning, had arranged the whole thing perfectly.

PRAYER LETTER

August 2001

Praise God! Kampi ya Samaki Child Care Centre officially opened and dedicated on August 11th 2001.

May God use it for his glory.

'The Lord will guide you always; he will satisfy your needs in a sun-scorched land and will strengthen your frame. You will be like a well-watered garden, like a spring whose waters never fail' (Isa. 58:11).

How true these words have been as I look back at the last months; hard ones in many ways, but times in which I've been very conscious of the Lord's presence, his ordering of every detail and giving strength for every task. We had a wonderfully happy day on August 11th when the Rev. Chirchir came to open the new Child Care Centre. The Committee did a great job organising it all, headed by Chairman Joel. Our chief, Patrick, was the Master of Ceremonies and friends from all over came to join us for the special occasion. The ladies cooked for 150 people! Rosemary drove round the lake to collect the children and housemothers from Kiserian and fifteen folk came up from Kajiado for the weekend.

It was very moving to hear the testimonies of Julius, the nurse in charge of Kajiado dispensary, and Keswe, another of our 'old boys' who has been through Daystar University, as well as Daniel Sapayia, all disabled following polio. Each one testified to how he had been made to feel useless as a child and yet, with God's help, had been able to become a useful and even leading member of society. It was a big help to have these young men inspire the Baringo Regional Church and community to identify physically disabled children and bring them for help.

Although I sought to emphasise the teamwork that had gone into the new Centre, including many gifts from the U.K. and many, many people praying, Rosemary and I had prayed specifically that the glory on the day would go to the Lord. I firmly believe He answered that prayer. Please pray that the glory continues to go to Him and that many children will come to know and love the Lord as a result of being helped there. We even managed to fit in some sightseeing over the weekend as the Kajiado folk had never seen flamingos or the hot springs at Lake Bogoria.

Other aspects of our ministry have gone on amid all the excitement and plans for the opening of the new Centre. Rosemary has continued teaching Bible Club at Kiserian each week and has helped with the Kampi Sunday School. We continue to do hospital trips and average at least 3,000 kilometres each month on some very bad and dangerous roads. Praise God for safety but keep on praying, as on our roads we certainly don't take safety for granted!

Five children continue to enjoy weekly visits to the spa pool at Bogoria Hotel for hydrotherapy and all have improved in mobility and confidence. Praise God that James can get in and out of the pool by himself, which is amazing considering that he couldn't even sit up three years ago. Pray for the mothers of these children, that they would look to the Lord for help with all the difficulties of caring for a physically disabled child in what is already a very difficult environment.

Pray especially for Esther, the mother of baby Georgie! Esther has a very difficult family situation but wonderfully gave her heart to the Lord a couple of months ago. Pray that she will grow ever closer to the Lord as she has devotions with her boys each day. Julius asked me to thank you for your prayers. He was accepted to do the course at Kijabe and started his training on August 13th. He asks you to pray for him, that he will be able to cope with the academic part of the course.

Praise God for the new mobile radio which is a big help, putting us in contact with other missionaries on the A.I.M. radio net at noon each day. And pray for me as I adjust to life without Rosemary who flew home on August 17th. Rosemary was the Lord's very special provision for me in this last, very action-packed year. Pray for her as she readjusts to life in Northern Ireland. I am going to miss her very much, not only for her work but also for the close fellowship we shared.

Thank you for your prayers,
Georgie.

14
Rosemary Gilmore remembers

When I arrived in Baringo I wondered how I was going to survive in such a hot climate! It was forty-seven miles from the Equator. Very little grows in the area, as it is semi-desert and a very dry, dusty and stony terrain. People have to work very hard to grow anything and keep animals in such a hostile environment. The local homes are very basic, small houses made out of mud walls and thatched roofs or mbatti (corrugated iron roofs). They have no electricity or running water in their homes. Early in the morning and at the end of the day children and women can be seen bent over with the weight of jerry cans as they carry water from the lake.

I first met Georgie Orme in 1993 when I went to help her in Kajiado for a few months. Right from the first day she welcomed me and involved me in her work with disabled children. Very quickly I realised how dedicated

Georgie was as she sought to help these boys and girls. It was very obvious to me that this wasn't just an ordinary job; God had given her a real love and ministry. In 1997 Georgie left the work she had established at Kajiado and moved to Baringo, a remote area, six hours drive north of Kajiado. I went to work as a volunteer with her in this new ministry in 2000 for a year and then as a short-term missionary in 2003 for two years.

When Georgie first moved from Kiserian to the other side of Lake Baringo she rented a fisherman's house just outside Kampi ya Samaki, a small village on the edge of Lake Baringo. I heard from other missionaries that the house was in an awful state when she first got it. The house had a veranda, a tiny strip of a kitchen and two very small rooms. Georgie gave up her personal space to have me live with her. Her living room/office became my bedroom and the veranda was our living room although most of the time we sat outside. I felt so much at home.

At the side of the house were two water tanks for storing rain water to be used for drinking and washing etc. This was our only source of water, neither was there electricity, though Georgie had invested in a solar panel for lighting. The shower and choo (toilet) were outside, behind the house. The choo wasn't the flushing kind, but it had a raised toilet seat, though it was a long drop (basically a hole in the ground). We had a solar camp shower, a strong plastic bag with a shower hose on the end. After a hot and busy day a shower was very welcome. The shower bag had to be filled every day and the water was usually the right temperature as the sun had heated it. Problems occurred during the heavy rains when everywhere was very muddy and swampy. There was a row of stones between the house and the shower/toilet but it was difficult to keep balance on the stones without slipping and getting very muddy after a shower! In fact, it was impossible ever to have clean feet.

One evening I was visiting the toilet before going to bed and heard rustling noises from the side of the house. I shone my torch thinking it was just lizards, but got the shock of my life to see a huge snake at the same spot where Georgie had been bitten by a black mamba! Thankfully, by the time Georgie came to my rescue, I had frightened the snake off into the bush! Georgie's response was, 'Now you'll believe me there are snakes here!' 'Of course I believed you! I can see the scar of the snake-bite on your hand!' I assured her. During my stay in Baringo I did see quite a few snakes around Georgie's house and on several occasions found snakes skins beside the toilet and shower! We had many other very unwelcome visitors inside the house such as rats and scorpions. The senior missionary killed them while the junior missionary screamed and was then assigned to remove the dead body! When we mentioned to the local people about our problems with rats they smiled and gave us a stick to kill them!

We never tired of the spectacular view over the lake. Often we could see fishermen in little canoe-shaped boats made out of reeds. Along the shores of the lake, crocodiles could often be seen and though the house was high above the lake, sometimes we found hippos' footprints outside and in the evening we could hear their distant grunts. Every morning we were wakened by the various choruses *of beautiful coloured birds. One of the 400 different species that live in the area actually sounds like an alarm clock! Sometimes we threw banana and watermelon skins outside and watched with delight as the monkeys came for a snack, often with mothers feeding their babies. We regularly treated the house with Gladiator poison to protect it from termites that could eat their way through an untreated house! There was so much wildlife we often laughed and said, 'Who needs TV?'*

By the time I came on the scene many strong relationships had been formed among the disabled children and their families. I automatically became their friend because I knew Georgie and I was treated like royalty. They all appreciated what Georgie sought to do for their children. I was touched by their kindness as they often showered us with gifts of watermelons, papaya, eggs etc. Every gift was special as I realised that they often struggled to make ends meet.

Driving was often a nightmare, especially in the rainy season. Several of the bridges that we had to cross had been completely destroyed by a flash flood. This meant we were diverted to driving across the very stony and dry riverbeds. In the rainy season it was a different story. Even though it might not be raining with us, if it had rained in the mountains, a dry riverbed could be waist deep in water in a matter of minutes. We had to be so careful if we were out in the bush that we were not stranded. Sometimes we found ourselves on the way home at the wrong side of a full river with a vehicle full of disabled children.

Georgie discovered a spa pool fed by hot springs at Lake Bogoria and decided it would be a good idea to use

Rosemary with Kandi in the
pool doing hydrotherapy

this local resource for hydrotherapy. Every week we collected children, very disabled due to cerebral palsy, and their mothers either from their homes or at the side of the road. The trip took about an hour and a half each way.

It was wonderful to see the children having so much freedom in the warm water. As well as doing hydrotherapy exercises we had lots of fun together singing, playing ball games and having races. The mothers were a great help with all the children and not just their own child. As these women were very isolated this became a time for talking, sharing and helping each other. The children always loved lunch! Not only did they get a plateful of chips each, but they were allowed to choose their fizzy drink! Drinking the soda was also a form of therapy, sucking through a straw! The first week the children couldn't manage to eat all their chips and insisted on taking them home. By the second week every single plate was clean! Although these days were busy and exhausting, they were special and worthwhile because the hydrotherapy made such a difference to the children. As Georgie and I look back we are so thankful for the improvement in the children's mobility and confidence.

Nearly every week Georgie took disabled children to a hospital at Kikuyu on the outskirts of Nairobi. The roads leaving Nairobi heading north are death traps. They are full of potholes and no one obeys any rules; it is really survival of the fittest. As this is the main road to Uganda there are always buses, lorries and heavy vehicles travelling along it. They overtake on corners and narrow parts of the road at crazy speeds, often cutting straight in and narrowly avoiding oncoming traffic. I saw a number of major accidents.

My first hospital safari (a safari is a journey in Kenya) with Georgie was very eventful! We left home at 6 a.m. to begin the four hour journey south to P.C.E.A. Kikuyu Hospital and picked up disabled children and their mothers, who were waiting at various points along the road. We had two unexpected stops. One of the children had serious travel sickness; Georgie always kept a tin bucket and toilet roll in the car. Then we had a puncture! Georgie also had major problems getting money from the bank to pay for the hospital fees. We arrived over an hour later than planned. Most of the day was spent with the doctor who assessed children at hospital for the first time and reviewed others. Daniel Sapayia brought some girls and boys who had been at Kajiado for rehabilitation and were ready to go home to Baringo. On the return journey the Land Cruiser was packed full of disabled children and their mothers, their small bags of belongings, calipers and crutches. The driver had the best seat! Georgie did this hospital trip regularly by herself, driving eight hours and having a busy day at hospital with all the surprises along the way! She was then twice my age, yet I was totally shattered.

One of our passengers was Timateo. He was a tall, lanky boy of about fifteen, severely disabled due to cerebral palsy. Timateo, who had major surgery on his *hips and legs, had been in hospital for several months. His uncle stayed with him during that time, learning to care for him post surgery, for example, being shown how to put his calipers on. As we drew close to the area where Timateo lived, I couldn't see anything that looked like a side road, just a very dry and dusty area with a narrow pathway between bushes. There were no signs of life and no houses to be seen. Timateo's uncle carried him through the bush until he was out of sight. There was no way that we could drive any nearer his house as it wasn't possible for a vehicle to pass through the thorny bushy area. I wondered where the boy's house was.*

A few days later Georgie and I returned with a wheelchair. Children seemed to appear from nowhere, which proved to be useful as they were able to show us to Timateo's home. We followed the children through the dry, bushy and very thorny area. On several occasions we stopped as we caught the thorn bushes on our clothes or stood on thorns which had come right through our sturdy sandals. The children were walking in bare feet without any problems! After about twenty minutes walk I could see in the distance a small round mud hut and little shelter made with a corrugated iron roof, all enclosed within a circle of thorn bushes to protect the animals. Timateo was outside lying in the dust on a piece of old rag in the shade of the roof surrounded by chickens and goats. It was great to see that his uncle had made parallel bars using iron piping as Georgie had instructed. She always tried to involve the family as much as possible with the care and rehabilitation of their child so that they felt responsible and realised that they had a vital role to play.

Timateo's uncle put on his calipers and boots and carried him to the parallel bars. The boy really struggled, but he did manage to walk a short distance. As with all disabled children, it was difficult to watch him struggle to walk as he was obviously in pain. I knew it was for his own good and that with practice every day he would improve but I found myself wishing that he could have all the resources we have in the West. Yet I knew that if Georgie hadn't taken him to hospital and helped him he would have no hope. He was one of the fortunate young folk to have been given a chance and with hard work, one day might walk. Georgie left the wheelchair with Timateo. I was comforted knowing that at least he wouldn't have to lie on an old piece of scrap material in the dust.

On my next visit to assess Timateo's progress he was nowhere to be found. The door to his small round mud house was padlocked. As I peered through the spaces between the sticks of the thatched roof I couldn't believe what I saw! Timateo was lying in the middle of his house on a filthy rag surrounded by chickens. He was only wearing an old dirty very holey tee-shirt. His wheelchair was nowhere to be seen and there was little evidence to show he had been walking and it seemed that he wasn't being shown any care or compassion. I thought of all the Christian love and care he had been shown by Georgie and the medical folk at the hospital and at Kajiado. It just broke my heart to see him lying there alone. I felt so helpless, upset and angry that he had been left in that condition. I couldn't say very much to him as I was just learning Swahili, but worst of all I couldn't get near him to hold him or help him. After many visits and much effort, it was with great sadness and with broken hearts that the decision was made that our efforts were wasted. It appeared that his uncle had disappeared and Timateo's only carer was a drunken old grandmother who left him alone for long periods. No one had been following any of the instructions to help him use his calipers or wheelchair. While we praised God for the hundreds of disabled young people who, through love and care, had been helped physically, and for the many who found spiritual healing in Christ, it was very hard to accept the disappointments.

Sitting at Georgie's farewell service in June 2005 I reflected over the past two years. All our dreams and hopes for the work at Baringo had seemed to be completely shattered when, due to ill health, Georgie had to leave. Although she was getting the best medical care in Nairobi, and had the pastoral care of the Mission, I found it difficult to leave her and return to Baringo alone. As I sat in the evenings I missed her for her wisdom and advice but most of all for her friendship and fellowship and being able to share the disappointments and joys.

Initially I was overwhelmed as I found myself working alone with the responsibility of handing over the Centre to the local church, a scenario I had never imagined and for which I had no training. Very quickly I realised that Georgie had been planning ahead and had already set many procedures in place. She had given the staff at the Child Care Centre many responsibilities. A small, dedicated, caring Committee was well established and already functioning well and were very enthusiastic. It was a joy to work with them as we learned together. Everyone in Baringo was very concerned and upset about Georgie and continually asked when she was returning.

It was difficult for them to accept that she would never be able to work in Baringo again. They were overjoyed when she returned briefly to say Farewell.

Georgie has been so much more than my senior missionary; she was my mentor, encourager, teacher, adviser and good friend. The Lord has honoured all her effort and dedication as the work in Kajiado and Baringo continues, showing God's love through caring for very needy disabled children.

15
From our loving Father's hand

'When everything around you seems to be shaking, dwell on the things that are certain.' I can almost hear Miss Norah Vickers voice, way back in my missionary training college days. 'There will be times when the only thing you are sure of is that you are truly God's child. If you are sure you are in the place God wants you to be, you will also know that everything that happens to you comes through the hands of our Heavenly Father, who loves you very much.' I have often had occasion to remember those wise words and have taken comfort from them.

That thought, plus the knowledge from God's Word that he intends everything for my good and his glory, made hard times easier to bear. The picture of God as a silversmith (Malachi 3) is very precious. He ensures that the furnace is hot enough to destroy all impurities, but not so hot that it will destroy the silver. I could see difficult times, at least in retrospect, as part of the answer to my rather naively prayed request in missionary training college, 'Lord, make me more like Jesus.' I didn't realise then what a painful process that would be.

When due to serious health problems the doctors said it would be dangerous for me to go back up into the heat of Kampi, it came as a thunderbolt. It seemed a complete reversal of all that I thought God had been saying to me about the handover of the work of Kampi Child Care Centre. The Management Committee and the staff had done really well during my home assignment and I returned to find everything going like clockwork. Another couple of years would see it running completely independently.

Rosemary and I rejoiced in God's perfect timing. He had brought her to help me as a short-term missionary for two years. I hadn't even thought of praying for someone to come and help me because I knew the time of handover to the Management Committee would be very short. When Rosemary said she felt that God was leading her to come until I retired I praised him, thinking, 'God knows I need help.' What God knew and I didn't, was that I wasn't even going to be there!

It was unthinkable to leave Rosemary to live alone in my house although I was sure that the chief and all the many who had cared for me so well would also care for her. I could see apprehension etched on her face as we faced her position together. The one thing she had said she couldn't do, she was now left to do

– the handover of leadership and the administration. Our plan had been for her to do all the physically tiring work like the driving, while I concentrated on the administration, putting all the money matters in place and keeping things going at home.

We missionaries of the far-flung Baringo District were very close. We had a supportive network and met for prayer once a month. Not everyone made it every time because of the huge distances, but we were aware of each other's needs and concerns, both personal and ministry. Most of us were on the A.I.M. radio net, and it was a rule that we reported in at noon each day. Rosemary was well used to doing that. Because ours was a mobile unit in the vehicle, help, in an emergency, was never far away.

Judi Troutman, the first ever woman A.I.M. Branch Executive Officer in Kenya, was a tower of strength to both of us in different ways. Having retired to the cooler clime of Nairobi, I was fighting like a tigress to keep my independence. But gradually, after increasing health problems, I realised that I was more of a liability than an asset. On the mission field the sense of family in A.I.M. is very strong. Leaving was like a bereavement. I had nowhere to go. Since my mother died I had had no home base in the U.K.. There is a limit to the number of doorsteps you can turn up on when you are as ill as I was at that point. After I left Kenya my 'family' and those I was closest to were on a different continent.

My pastor was a tremendous support and found me several places to stay, but all the moves and the packing and unpacking were beginning to take their toll. 'Lord, please, just take me to heaven; it would be so much simpler.' At least I knew for sure I had a place there. But gradually my prayer changed as I realised that to get to heaven I would have to die first. It would not be very nice for any of my hostesses to have me die in her house! My prayer changed to, 'Lord please give me a place of my own to die in!'

Gradually my varied health problems were getting sorted out, but I found myself longing for that which I had found so trying in my early missionary days. In Kenya, when one was ill, the whole world came to pray, to say sorry and to bring small gifts of tea or sugar or some honey. I used to think, 'I wish people would just leave me alone to die in peace.' Now I longed for people to come because I didn't have the energy to reach out to others. The Scottish way of caring is different – you don't intrude; you keep yourself to yourself. I was lonely. I had become used to the sense of community in Kenyan culture and I missed it terribly.

Worse than that, the God whom I loved and served seemed a million miles away. I knew in my head he wasn't, but I didn't feel it in my heart. God supplied me, through friends, with a lovely little sheltered retirement flat rent-free! Some friends bought me a bed, other friends brought furniture. But although the evidence of God's love and grace surrounded me I had no sense of his presence. God supplied me with everything I needed. Why did my heart feel so cold? Why was I so fearful? I was gripped by a fear of losing my independence, which at one point looked quite likely.

One day I was reading a passage in James 5, which I had read many times before. It was, 'Is any one of you sick? He should call the elders of the church to pray over him and anoint him with oil in the name of the Lord.' The thought came into my mind. 'Do it.' It's not a very Presbyterian thing to do, but I was desperate. It was such an encouragement to me when the elders came. Even the concern they showed by coming meant a lot. I was anointed with oil and then each one prayed for me. I felt the healing peace of God just flood into my heart. The fear went and I knew that, whatever the days ahead held, God was with me in them.

Barry Douglas, who was the new A.I.M. Scottish Director, was a tremendous support. And, as time passed and I gained strength, he encouraged me to go back to Kenya to say goodbye properly. It had been a wrench to leave Kampi in the way I did, although I knew that Rosemary had done a really good job in handing over the work. So it was great to be able to go and see everybody for myself. Rosemary drove me up and we were made a fuss of and given many gifts.

At Kajiado, unknown to me, a huge ceremony was planned. Many people came, representatives from all the years and various ministries of which I had been part. As I saw Daniel confidently taking the lead, having organised that huge event, I couldn't help but think back to my first meeting with him as he sat in his little booth in Kajiado town trying to make a living from shoe repairs. How good it was that we didn't know what lay ahead. My reaction, and I'm sure Daniel's too, would have been, 'I can't do that! I am not trained for any of it.' Yet over the years God had led us, slowly but surely, step by step, either bringing people to tell us what we needed to know, or opening up opportunities for us to go to other places to get the knowledge. I knew that the God who led us so lovingly and carefully over the years would continue to lead Daniel and the children in his ways.

Many of my old boys and girls attended the goodbye ceremony – children I had cared for from two or three years old, now confident adults and doing well in their chosen professions. Most of them I hadn't seen for many years. Stephen Kimendere had been a huge help in the early days of the Child Care Centre. He was a mature boy who made his own way to us, even persuading the ticket collector on the train from Magadi to Kajiado to let him travel free. Because he had experienced rejection by his family he was grateful to find a caring new home and he had a way of getting alongside other younger boys and supporting them. Kimendere was also a tremendous help maintaining

discipline. He helped in all sorts of ways, even to organising the Saturday cleaning jobs. He was almost like another member of staff. I greatly missed him when he went away to secondary school. I admired his initiative and great stick-ability in overcoming his disabilities.

After completing secondary schooling Kimendere went back to Magadi to the primary

Kimendere preparing to leave for Teacher Training College.

school in his home area. There he was employed as an untrained nursery school teacher. He did so well, in spite of his crutches, that he got a place in a teacher training college. When he graduated he was posted back to the same school. Most teachers were reluctant to work in such difficult areas, but Kimendere was happy to go because it had been home. He was promoted to be deputy headmaster, and finally headmaster. At first his family, other teachers, the community and even the pupils, had a really negative attitude toward his disability. But he kept working hard and patiently and had great faith in God. Eventually his patience was rewarded and he was accepted and became a respected leader in that society. Stephen Kimendere is now the main breadwinner in his family and is assisting his able-bodied brothers and sisters in their education.

People are always amazed when they see a child walking who had previously only been able to crawl. I must say I was pretty amazed myself at what my 'wee' children had achieved. True, I had been able to help them physically. When they left us at the end of primary schooling I struggled to find places for them in secondary schools or training in some skill. Mostly I had to help with finance too, but all the effort was theirs. They often faced rejection and frustration, and yet they persevered in making a place for themselves in life. I thought back to words that meant a lot to me in the early days. 'The people were amazed when they saw ... the lame walking. ... And they praised the God of Israel' (Matt.15:31).

Of course, I was the focus of that day as it was my

farewell party, but the emphasis in all the speeches and testimonies was praise to the God of Israel who had made it all possible. I was amazed at the work that had gone into the celebrations. The church was beautifully decorated. Goats had been slaughtered to feed the crowds and many people made speeches. It was all so well arranged. A wonderful surprise! I was presented with numerous gifts. The main one from my 'old' boys and girls was a batik – a beautifully coloured cloth painting of Maasai women, with children crawling and hopping. In presenting it to me this is how Julius explained it. 'This is us when we were brought to Child Care Centre crawling. And this is us after we were treated, able to run and skip and play football.'

Playing football

I thought back to Julius when I first met him. He was part-way through secondary school, about to drop out because of a huge debt. His parents had no hope of being able to raise the money for his school fees. Julius had to walk with one hand pressing on his thigh to support his paralysed leg so that it wouldn't collapse under him. One of the teachers had approached me to see if I could find help with his fees. At that time Julius joined our other secondary school boys when they went to a Word of Life camp. It was there that he became a Christian. I especially remember when he was doing the Word of Life's three-month Bible school while anxiously waiting for the results of the Kenya Certificate of Secondary Education. He did extremely well and came to me very seriously and said, 'Naado, I believe God is calling me to be a nurse.' My heart sank. How could a disabled boy be a nurse? He went on, 'God has helped me so much I want to repay him by serving him as a nurse.' Julius was certain that is what God wanted him to do.

When I thought further about it I realised that the only real problem would be getting through his training. After that he could work in a dispensary and wouldn't need to walk the miles in wards that he would need to do in hospital nursing. Julius applied to Kijabe School of Nursing and, after a medical examination performed by our friend Dr Dick Bransford, he was accepted to start training. Having successfully qualified as a Kenya Enrolled Community Health Nurse, he later upgraded to a Kenya Registered Community Health nurse, and was put in charge of the Kajiado A.I.C. Dispensary, which operates in the Child Care Centre compound.

Julius with a patient in Kajiado dispensary

One of the highlights of the ceremony for me was when Kakayon, our old choirmaster, now a schoolteacher, led the reunited Child Care Centre choir in my favourite song.

*Eishoo Enkai iyiook ntirman, te nkang ang, te nkang
  e Yesu.*
God gives us crutches in our home, the home of
  Jesus.
God gives us love in our home, the home of Jesus.
God gives us peace in our home, the home of Jesus.

As they sang 'God gives us crutches,' they waved their crutches proudly in the air. I remembered them doing that when they were very small children, years before, when they were invited to sing at a ceremony in Nairobi. It moved me then as it still does now.

Of all the many speeches one that sticks in my mind, and there were many kind words said that day, is the one by Parsalunye. In it, this is what he said. 'As a child who was in the Child Care Centre, both when I was young and as I got older, I must say that I feel privileged to have been born of two loving mothers, my biological mother and Naado, who brought me up for a period not less than sixteen years. Friends, I know many of those who have experienced the motherly love and care of Naado. Brothers and sisters, Naado, whom I referred to as 'mother', is indeed a mother and a 'father' as well. She has been caring, loving and always concerned for us. She nurtured her children physically and mentally and spiritually. For instance, I can remember several occasions when we used to have home visits, going to Maasai villages to preach. I remember her taking us to Word of Life camp for spiritual nourishment, and also going on tours to Mombasa, where she could share experiences of life with us. Surely Mum, we shall miss you very much.'

As I listened to his sincere words, I was reminded of the verses I was given by an Anglican Canon away back in 1975, verses he believed was God's word to him describing what my future ministry would be. *'We were gentle among you, like a mother caring for her little children. We loved you so much that we were delighted to share with you not only the gospel of God but our lives as well, because you had become so dear to us.'* At the time I highlighted the words in my Bible, but doubted they were really for me. Looking around the smiling faces that day I could apply every part of those verses to my life and ministry and know them to be true. My dear children were all around me and it had been my delight, in the strength of the Lord alone, to care for them as a mother and to share with them the gospel of God and his love. In the crowd I saw too, members of their families and folk from their communities, many reached for the gospel through the care we, the staff, none of us trained for the work, had been able to give. And as I left Kenya for the last time I praised God for the witness of the children, remembering the poor wee scraps who had been brought to me years before. God had done amazing things in them and through them and together we had all proved him gloriously true to his word, 'My grace is sufficient for you, for my power is made perfect in weakness.'

UNAFRAID
OF THE
SACRED FOREST

THE BIRTH OF A CHURCH IN AN AFRICAN TRIBE

RONALDO LIDORIO

Unafraid of the Sacred Forest:
The Birth of a Church in an African Tribe
Ronaldo Lidorio

Ghana is considered one of the success stories of West Africa. Its government is relatively stable and the widespread use of English, as part of its colonial heritage, gives it easier access to the world at large. If Ronaldo and Rossana Lidorio were expecting a lightly Westernised African state when they went to the north of Ghana as missionaries such preconceptions were soon dispelled. They came up against formidable cultural and language barriers, illiteracy and human sacrifice. Where would you start if you entered a society where there are only 6 days to the week and no such thing as a year (and consequently no birthdays)? Where polygamy is a virtue and sisters are regularly swapped? Where the most powerful person in the village is not the tribal chief but the Witch Doctors, who have practiced their art for thousands of years? One of the themes, as you read this exciting story of modern missionary endeavour, is the counter-cultural one of 'sacrifice'. Ronald and Rossana worked on the foundations of others who prepared the way and alongside similarly committed people. 17 churches have now been planted in this previously un-reached area and 81 church leaders trained. The Konkomba tribes are now sending their own evangelists into other areas to bring the Good News of Christ to more people.

Ronaldo & Rossana Lidorio are Brazilians who were missionaries in Northern Ghana for many years. Continuing their work amongst unreached nations.

ISBN 978 1 84550 235 5

For reviews of this book, visit www.christianfocus.com

Is There Anybody Out There?
A Journey from Despair to hope
Mez McConnell

Since the publication of 'A child called "it"' by Dave Pelzer there hasn't been a story like this.

But this is not just another harrowing story about an excruciating childhood and the ravages on a life it produces. The difference is that Mez not only escaped from his 'trial by parent' but he discovered a hope that has transformed his life. He in turn has helped others find hope in their lives.

Mez's story is told with a frankness and wit that hides much of the pain and despair that was his everyday experience. Nevertheless, although his story at times may sicken you, his first brushes with the faith that restored him will make you laugh out loud!

Mez's life involved abuse, violence, drugs, thieving and prison - but you don't have to fall as far as him in order to climb out of the traps in your life.

Do you like happy endings? Mez still suffers from his experiences but you'll be amazed at how far you can be restored from such a beginning.

Mez McConnell is now a missionary with Unevangelised Fields Mission (UFM) working with street kids in Brazil. He is married with two children of his own.

ISBN 978 1 84500 205 8

YOU'LL GO TO LONDON
THE AUTOBIOGRAPHY OF LIONEL BALL

You'll Go to London
The Autobiography of Lionel Ball
Lionel Ball

Lionel Ball served as a London City Missionary most of his working life. A whole generation of London City Missionaries are grateful to God for the encouragement given to them by him. Even today, some years after his retirement, missionaries regularly meet people who ask, 'Do you remember Lionel Ball?'

Before coming to the mission he worked with the police, where he was so highly regarded that he was appointed a Freeman of the City of London. This meant that he could drive sheep across London Bridge without paying. There is no record of him ever taking advantage of the privilege. Instead Lionel was to undertake a different sort of shepherding!

The key place he worked was at the Covent Garden Mission, then a medical mission, but known locally as 'The Miracle Mission.' Lionel and others used to gather people into a room there and show the **Fact and Faith** Films.

Not unusually the room was filled with homeless men who were made to feel welcome by the open and generous welcome they received.

Lionel Ball was also involved in mission activity in the London theatres. Blessed with a fine voice, and himself a gifted pianist, he related well to performers and won their confidence and love. There are many who can trace their early Christian influence back to Lionel Ball.

Lionel Ball has spents years ganing the respect of Londoners in the Police Force through his work with the London City Mission. He is now retired but has been granted the freedom of the city.

ISBN 978 1 84550 314 7

IRENE HOWAT

A WEEK
IN THE LIFE OF

MAF

MISSION AVIATION
FELLOWSHIP

A Week in the Life of MAF
Mission Aviation Fellowship
Irene Howat

For five decades, Mission Aviation Fellowship (MAF) planes have been serving countless thousands of men, women and children, bringing medical care, emergency food, and Christian hope. In the places of deepest need they are serving as the air-arm of the church, enabling the work of aid and development agencies, missions, national churches and other local groups.

Using aircraft and electronic communication networks MAF overcomes barriers that isolate people from spiritual and physical help. These are remote places where flying is not a luxury but a lifeline. Operating over 130 aircraft from bases in 30 countries, today every three minutes, a MAF plane is taking off or landing somewhere in the world

Best selling author Irene Howat has compiled the accounts of MAF workers in the field and invites you to experience a week in their lives. Flying across deserts, jungles, mountains and swamps, be transported to some of the most inaccessible areas in the world with MAF employees who are giving hope to far-flung communities. From the Ecuadorian jungle to the wetlands of Bangladesh to the Mongolian plains prepare for take off on an exhilarating and eye opening journey that you will never forget.

ISBN 978 1 85792 940 9

For reviews of this book, visit www.christianfocus.com

Christian Focus Publications
publishes books for all ages

Our mission statement –

STAYING FAITHFUL
In dependence upon God we seek to help make His infallible Word, the Bible, relevant. Our aim is to ensure that the Lord Jesus Christ is presented as the only hope to obtain forgiveness of sin, live a useful life and look forward to heaven with Him.

REACHING OUT
Christ's last command requires us to reach out to our world with His gospel. We seek to help fulfil that by publishing books that point people towards Jesus and help them develop a Christ-like maturity. We aim to equip all levels of readers for life, work, ministry and mission.

Books in our adult range are published in three imprints.

Christian Focus contains popular works including biographies, commentaries, basic doctrine and Christian living. Our children's books are also published in this imprint.

Mentor focuses on books written at a level suitable for Bible College and seminary students, pastors, and other serious readers. The imprint includes commentaries, doctrinal studies, examination of current issues and church history.

Christian Heritage contains classic writings from the past.

Christian Focus Publications, Ltd
Geanies House, Fearn,
Ross-shire, IV20 1TW, Scotland, United Kingdom
info@christianfocus.com